Learning the
Joy of
Prayer

Keith Robertson

Learning the Joy of Prayer

How to spend one hour with God

Larry Lea
with Judy Doyle

Harvestime

Published in the United Kingdom by:
Harvestime Services Ltd, 12a North Parade, Bradford
West Yorkshire BD1 3HT

Copyright © 1987 Larry Lea
First published by Creation House 1987
This UK edition published by Harvestime Services Ltd
First printed October 1989

Scripture quotations are generally taken from the New
International Version. Copyright © 1978 by the New
York Bible Society and published by Hodder &
Stoughton.
Used by permission

Other versions referred to: King James Version (KJV)
Revised Authorised Version (RAV), Amplified Bible
(Amp)

British Library Cataloguing in Publication Data:

Lea, Larry
    Learning the joy of prayer.
    1. Christian life. Prayer
    I. Title II. Doyle, Judy
    248.3'2
ISBN 0-947714-76-6

Typeset by: E Thompson (Typesetters) Ltd.,
Bradford BD8 7BX
Reproduced, printed and bound in Great Britain by
BPCC Hazell Books Ltd
Member of BPCC Ltd
Aylesbury, Bucks, England

Contents

Part Seven: Praise
'Yours is the kingdom and the power and the glory
for ever'

Part Eight: Prerequisites, patterns, participation

Preface

In the cold, black night of Christ's betrayal, his disciples could not tarry one hour with him in prayer. In the Garden of Gethsemane, while Jesus earnestly prayed in such agony of spirit that his sweat became like great drops of blood falling to the ground, his disciples, ignorantly oblivious to the eternity-shaping events about to transpire, slept.

Jesus, heavy and sorrowful in spirit, awakened his sleeping disciples and asked, 'Could you men not keep watch with me for one hour?' (Matthew 26:40).

Mirrored in that tragic scene is the plight of the church today. Jesus, our interceding High Priest, is praying; his disciples are sleeping; and Satan is winning contest after contest by *default.*

It would be impossible to calculate the failures, the ruined reputations, the defeats, the broken homes and the other multiplied tragedies that could have been avoided if believers had prayed. It would be impossible to measure the destruction that could have been turned and the judgment that might have been averted if only God's people had taken the time to pray. I am guilty, and so are you.

But I didn't write this book to send anybody on a guilt trip. I wrote it because I know what it's like to be haunted by the call to pray, and because I know what it's like to let interruptions, fatigue and pressures drown out that call. You see, God haunted me for six years with the call to pray before I finally obeyed his plea to tarry with him one hour each day in prayer. But when I did so, my life and ministry were revolutionised.

I want to make you a promise: something supernatural happens when you pray an hour a day. It does not happen overnight, but slowly, almost imperceptibly, the *desire* to pray becomes firmly planted in the soil of your heart by the Spirit of God. This desire crowds out the weeds of apathy and neglect, and matures into the *discipline* to pray. Then one day you discover that prayer is no longer just a duty or drudgery; instead, the discipline of prayer has borne the fruit of *delight*. You find yourself eagerly longing for your daily time with God.

The supernatural work of prayer continues and begins to possess and reshape every area of your life. You notice that your heart is no longer devoid of the presence and promises of God. You discover how to set, maintain and pray God's priorities in your life; you learn how to appropriate God's provision for your needs. Life moves into a new dimension as you begin to experience greater joy and fulfilment in your relationships with people.

And as you begin to walk, not in the realm of the flesh, but in the realm of the Spirit, you discover how to move in the power of God and stand in the victory Jesus has won for you.

How do I know? I know because that is what happened to me as I obeyed the call to pray. I know because that is what happened to the believers after Christ's ascension.

Think about it: what transformed the slumbering disciples, disheartened believers and vacillating followers pictured in the final chapters of the gospels into the determined, driving, unified army of the book of Acts? What made them into a mighty, spiritual army that seized difficulties and turned them into opportunities; an army characterised by clear-headed, incisive decisions instead of foggy thinking and confusion; an army that, in one generation, turned the world upside down for Jesus Christ?

Prayer. Prayer that unleashed the power of God and tapped into his infinite resources.

What will transform the slumbering disciples, disheartened believers and vacillating followers today into a mighty, marching army with deliverance as its song and healing in its hands?

Prayer. Prayer that snatches the victories Jesus won for us out of Satan's greedy clutches. Prayer that storms the gates of hell.

If you do not consistently pray one full hour every day but would like to learn how, take the prayer secrets the Holy Spirit has taught me on my knees and begin to practise them. As you learn to pray the way Jesus taught us to pray, your prayer life will no longer be a frustrating, hit-or-miss experience; instead, tarrying with the Lord an hour in prayer will actually become easy and natural.

Won't you bow your head right now and pray: 'Jesus, plant in my heart the desire to pray. Enable me to develop a daily, consistent time of prayer. Transform prayer from a duty to a delight. Make me a mighty warrior in your prayer army'?

Did you pray that prayer? Did you mean it? Then you had better get your uniform out of mothballs, polish those brass buttons and shine your boots because, soldier, God's army is getting ready to march.

Larry Lea

Part One

Preparation

1

His name is not Henry

I was seventeen years old in 1968 when the heavy doors of the psychiatric ward of Mother Frances Hospital in Tyler, Texas, closed and locked behind me.

I had a brand new convertible and a beautiful girl-friend; I was an all-state golfer with a scholarship; I lived in a large house. (The entire second floor was mine — two bedrooms, two bathrooms and a study.) I had a lot of 'stuff'. But I went stark-raving crazy in that environment because I had everything on the outside and nothing on the inside.

Weeks before, I had sought help from my dad, who had made his money in the oil and gas business in Texas.

'Help me, Dad!' I begged.

But my father was an alcoholic who didn't know Jesus; his heart was as empty as mine. All he did was stare at me for a moment in disbelief, then exclaim in exasperation, 'Larry, any kid who has everything you've got and is depressed has got to be on drugs.'

My mother, who was a Christian, rushed to my defence. 'My son wouldn't get on drugs,' she retorted, shocked by my father's accusation. 'He must have a brain tumour or something.'

During this terrible time of depression, I went to church one Sunday morning looking for something real. I needed help so badly that at the end of the service I walked to the front of the church — watched by all my friends seated on the back row. I said to the pastor, 'Sir, have you got anything for me? I'm losing my mind, and I don't know what's wrong.'

Do you know what the pastor did? He just patted me on the shoulder and whispered reassuringly, 'You'll be all right, son. You're a good boy. Here, fill out this card.'

All Dad had to offer me was money, and all the church had for me was a card to fill out. I didn't know anywhere else to turn, so when my mother kept insisting that something must be physically wrong with me, I gave in and went to the doctor. After extensive tests revealed no physical reason for my deep emotional problems, I was admitted to a hospital psychiatric ward, and the rounds of psychological examinations began.

Soon the doctor walked into my room and said in an understanding tone, 'You're depressed, aren't you? These will help.'

He handed me four tranquillisers, and the next thing I knew, every four hours someone brought me four little pills. That did it: I lost it. The last lights of reality flickered out, and the fog rolled in. The doctors called it a nervous breakdown, but in reality it was a 'transgression breakdown'. I was a sinner who didn't understand Christ's atonement for sin. I didn't know life could have purpose.

For six weeks in that ward I didn't even see the sun. Part of the time I lay in a drugged stupor with my eyes rolled back in my head. When I would come to, I thought the black lady cleaning the floor was my mother and that the patient across the hall was the doctor. There I was, the heir to a fortune, and I had lost my mind.

My grief-stricken parents reluctantly made reservations at the state mental hospital so I could be committed.

But before I could be transferred, one day I strayed out of my room into the hall, where I noticed a crucifix. Being somewhat curious, I removed it from the wall and managed to focus my eyes and thoughts long enough to make out its Latin inscription, *INRI*. Confused, I wandered along the corridors of that Catholic hospital, collecting crucifixes and pondering those puzzling letters.

Of course, when the nuns spied me with the crucifixes clutched to my chest, they rushed forward to retrieve them. With the sisters in hot pursuit, I broke into a run, and my befuddled muttering amplified into a bewildered wail, loud enough for the whole world to hear: 'His name is not Henry . . . . His name is not Henry! His name is Jesus!'

In my room several days later, I seemed to come to my senses. I fell to my knees and began to cry out, 'Jesus! Jesus! Merciful Jesus!' It was not a very religious prayer. I just called out to God over and over, pleading, weeping, sobbing out his name.

Suddenly, I heard an inner voice speak in my spirit. He said, 'Now you are my son. You will take my message to this generation. You will be my mouthpiece and my minister.' Then the voice told me I could get up and go home.

I was well, but I couldn't leave because they had me locked up. The doctor came in the next day and asked routinely, 'How are you doing, Larry?'

'I'm better now,' I answered.

Puzzled, the doctor hesitated, then asked matter-of-factly, 'Why do you think you're better now?'

Returning his steady gaze, I said, 'Because yesterday I talked to God.'

The doctor raised his eyebrow and muttered sceptically, 'Yes, right.' But unable to deny the peace that had replaced my inner turmoil, he soon discharged me from the hospital.

That psychiatric ward was a strange place to begin my walk with the Lord. But when I cried out to him, Jesus came through the locked doors and barred windows: he walked right into my heart and placed a call on my life to serve my generation. Like a newborn colt on weak, wobbling legs, I walked out of the hospital and back into life. But this time I didn't walk alone. Since that hour, I've never been out of his care.

Why am I willing to open the dusty pages of my life and share that story with you? Because my misery is forgotten — passed away — and in its place abides steady peace and divine purpose. I believe *you* are part of that purpose. God has drawn us together in order that you might partake of the grace he has extended to me.

I don't know at which juncture my experiences will interface with yours or at what point the word of the Lord will come to you, but it will happen — and the truth will set you free. Constraining habits that keep you from God's best, obsolete ways of seeing yourself or others, lifeless traditions that exert control over you even though truth long ago overpowered them — all will be defied by the Spirit of God who makes all things new.

I invite you to partake of my grace and to learn, from the Holy Spirit's gentle, friendly instruction, what I have learned through the painful yet precious experiences of my life.

How about you? Is your situation as desperate as mine was? Are you in a place where you can't talk or buy your way out, and there's no back door? Perhaps you're not there; perhaps you're just in the spiritual doldrums. Nothing seems new anymore. You were saved years ago and now you're sure you've 'heard it all'.

'Since when,' you say sceptically, 'has God said anything new to anybody?'

Well, let me give you some advice: stop trying to think your problem through or wait it through. Pray it through.

Your *situation* may or may not be desperate, but only

when *you* are desperate enough to get down on your knees, confess your needs to him and call on his name will he speak peace to you and your problems. That's your next step. Take it now, my friend. Take it now.

And when you call out to him, remember: his name is not Henry. His name is Jesus!

2

A radical change

Almost two decades have passed since that day in the psychiatric ward when I wept my way into Christ's presence and his peace flooded my being.

I know now what healed me. For the first time in my life I comprehended that God saw me right where I was and knew me, that he needed me and had a purpose for my life and that I needed him.

These same three needs are basic to every human being, including you. You need *somebody to see you;* you need *somebody to need you;* you need *something to give your life to.* Giving your life to another human being is not enough. Pouring yourself into a career and buying material things will not feed the gnawing need in your heart. There will always be a 'vacancy' sign flashing in the window of your soul.

When I discovered Jesus, life seemed to pulse with purpose and meaning. I couldn't keep it to myself. I had to share what I had discovered. But there was a problem. Pastors wouldn't let me preach in the churches because they thought I had 'nuthouse religion', so I preached at the ice-cream parlour or wherever anybody would listen.

I finally got my chance, though, when they agreed to let me preach just once at First Baptist Church in Kilgore, Texas, my hometown.

That Sunday a hippy sat listening to me preach. I knew by his vacant stare that either his brain was fried or he was stoned out of his mind right there in church. Sometime during the service I realised that the hippy was Jerry Howell, the keyboard player for a rock band

called The Mouse and the Traps. (Jerry was one of
the Traps.) The group had a number-one song on the
Dallas charts at that time. The local kids idolised
Jerry, but their parents thought he was the scourge
of the earth.

At the end of the service, Jerry walked up to me and
remarked casually, 'I really related to what you said
today.'

'Jerry, what are you doing in church, man?' I asked
as I shook his outstretched hand.

He sighed. 'Well, my dad died six months ago, and
I promised him on his deathbed that I'd drive back
from the University of Texas every weekend and take
my brother to church. I'm just keeping my word to my
dad.'

Jerry paused and lowered his voice. 'What you had
to say is the first thing I've heard here in the last six
months that's made any sense to me.'

Later, I couldn't get Jerry off my mind. I knew he
was reaching out for help, so I phoned and asked him
to go to church with me.

'Jerry,' I began hesitantly, 'er . . . this is Larry Lea.'

Dead silence on the other end of the line.

'Er, Jerry . . . I'm a youth director now at the First
Baptist Church in New London.' (I didn't add that it
was the only Baptist church in the tiny town.)

'Jerry,' I continued more confidently, 'why don't you
come out and play the organ for me? You can play
Amazing Grace, can't you? I'll sing and you can play,
and we'll have church with all these young people.'

'*Me?*' he answered. 'You want *me* to play organ in
a *church?*'

Little did I know that every day for four years Jerry
Howell had been high on drugs. I later learnt that
when the phone rang, Jerry had been out in his back
garden counting the blades of grass, trying to keep his
head on his shoulders.

'Look, Jerry, I need your help,' I assured him. 'You

have a great talent, and God can use you. He loves you, man, and he has a plan for your life. I'll drive by and get you this evening. I'll even get you a date,' I added, waiting for his reply.

'A date!' he blurted. 'With a church girl?'

At seven o'clock I went to pick up Jerry for the service. He was dressed in his faded blue jeans and a tee-shirt. He had blond hair flowing down to his waist but was bald on top. And his old van — the kind with drawn curtains on the windows and an elaborate stereo system blaring Jimi Hendrix and Led Zeppelin rock — was in the driveway.

Here I sat with my short-back-and-sides haircut, my tape of Jim Nabors singing *The Lord's Prayer* and the family Bible on the dashboard. When Jerry climbed into my car, his eyes darted from the family Bible, to me, back to the Bible, then straight ahead. Boy, was he quiet. We drove and picked up the girls, but Jerry hardly said a word to anybody.

As we stepped inside the church, I nodded my head towards the platform and said, 'Jerry, there's the organ. You know what to do.'

Jerry played *Amazing Grace* in a way it's never been played before or since! I sang and preached, and we had church.

It was about eleven-thirty when we pulled into his driveway after dropping the girls off. Jerry spoke for practically the first time all evening.

'Larry, is there anything to this Jesus?' he asked earnestly.

I hardly knew how to respond because Jerry was confused, in the middle of a nervous breakdown and bound with drugs, but I breathed a prayer for help.

During the first part of our conversation that night, Jerry asked a lot of questions that I didn't have the answers to. Sometimes I honestly replied, 'I don't know, Jerry.' But God filled my mouth, and I just kept giving him Jesus.

When we got through talking, it was three-thirty in the morning. Jerry stared straight ahead, heaved a deep sigh and asked, 'Well, how do I get it?'

So I — deep Christian and experienced soulwinner that I was — said, 'What you do is, you open your Bible to Matthew five, six and seven [because that was the only part of the Bible I knew], then you get on your knees and start hollering, "Jesus! Jesus! Jesus!" and when it hits you, you'll know you've got it.'

That night Jerry Howell did just that, but before he could hit his knees, God had saved him, delivered him from a four-year drug habit and called him to preach.

When it was over, Jerry walked to the home of his best friend, Max, the drummer for their band. It was six o'clock on the fourth of July, and Max was out in the back garden feeding his rabbits. (These were strange people.)

When Jerry came around the corner of the house, Max took one look at him and gasped, 'Man, what happened to you?'

Jerry grinned and explained, 'I met this weird little dude named Larry Lea, and we talked all night about Jesus.'

'Hey, man, how do I get it?'

Jerry gave it to him straight. 'You get your Bible and you read Matthew five, six and seven, then you get down on your knees and . . . .'

At seven-thirty that morning my phone rang. It was Jerry.

'Larry, I got it, I got it! And I came down here and told Max about it, and he got it, too. But you know how strange he is. You'd better come over here and check him out.'

That wasn't the only phone call Jerry Howell made that day. The local barber shop was closed for the holiday, but Jerry called the barber at home.

'Mr Buck,' he said hesitantly, 'this is Jerry Howell. Would you cut my hair?'

Mr Buck didn't stutter. Quick as a flash, he answered, 'Sure, son. Come on over.' He couldn't resist adding, 'I've been wanting to cut your hair for a long time.'

Six weeks later, a clean-shaven Jerry Howell with a short-back-and-sides haircut went off to Bible college with the weird little dude named Larry Lea. One day Jerry announced, 'Larry, God has called me to preach, and I'm supposed to go hold an evangelistic campaign.'

And that's exactly what he did. Within six months after his own conversion, Jerry Howell had led a thousand people to God!

Jerry is now pastor of Church on the Rock in Kilgore, Texas, the very place where he was once considered the offscouring of the earth. How did that radical change come about? You see, Jesus came along and said, '*I see you,* Jerry Howell, hiding there behind your walls, and *I need you* for a special task. I've got something you can give your life to. All I need to hear you say is that *you need me.*'

Now I want to ask an important question. How about you, my friend? Do you need a radical change in your heart? In your home? In your relationships? Are you sick of your doubts and unbelief? Jesus sees you right where you are. He needs you for something special that only you can do. And you need him.

Jesus changed Larry Lea, a seventeen-year-old boy in a psychiatric ward. Jesus changed a Texan hippy named Jerry Howell. And he can change you, too. You don't even have to read Matthew five, six and seven. Just get down on your knees and call on Jesus.

And don't worry: when it hits you, you'll know you got it!

3

Read the red and pray for the power

Jerry Howell and I, two growing, newborn converts, were room-mates at Dallas Baptist College. Besides attending class, about all we did for three years was 'read the red' and pray for the power. We devoured the words of Jesus that were printed in red ink in our black Bibles.

Jerry and I were captivated by Christ's miracles, compassion and power to help the helpless. We craved what he had. We longed to do what he did. We hungered and thirsted for more of Jesus.

One night I left the dorm and went for a walk. It was a still, clear night, and the view of the lights, mirrored in the lake in the valley below the college, was serene and soothing. I strolled along the edge of the hill and talked to God.

After a time, I paused and stared up at the stars, but the consuming desire in my heart stretched far beyond those shimmering pinpoints of light.

'Oh, God,' I pleaded, my face wet with tears, 'I want all you have for me. Please, Father, if there's power in this gospel, give it to me! Give it to me, Lord . . . .'

I guess you know it's dangerous to pray a prayer like that. The next thing I knew, my startled ears heard my stammering lips speaking a language I had never learned. Shocked, I clamped my hand over my mouth and gasped, 'But, God, we don't believe in this!'

Does that blow your theology? Don't worry; it blew mine, too. I didn't understand what had taken place, but it sounded an awful lot like what the disciples experienced in the book of Acts.

I didn't let it happen again for a while. But one evening I visited the home of a minister who prayed over me. Sure enough, my new prayer language came bubbling out again. This time I just let it flow. I knew this was the Holy Spirit and that he had filled and flooded my being in answer to that honest, desperate prayer. God also baptised Jerry in the Holy Spirit.

Although we tried not to be divisive or to make a big deal about our experiences, word about the two guys with the funny prayer languages soon got round to most of the four hundred budding Baptist preachers in our dorm. Their reactions were mixed: icy aloofness, warm interest, red-hot hostility and all in between.

At night when we knelt beside our beds and began to pray, we would hear doors creak open all along our hall. We would listen as scurrying feet stopped abruptly outside our door. One night Jerry rose quietly to his feet, crept stealthily across the floor and threw open the door. There, crouched at our threshold, were several surprised, embarrassed fellow-students.

We all had a good laugh about it, and the guys learned that even though Jerry and I, in the privacy of our room, sometimes prayed in prayer languages other than English, we weren't in there swinging from the light fixture or rolling on the floor. We were just experiencing praise and intercession in a powerful new dimension. And the guys who were interested soon discovered that we were willing to talk about our fulfilling new experience if they cared to risk it.

For a while it seemed that Jerry and I were going to get along well with most of those other Baptist preacher boys. But one of my professors at the college learned of my baptism in the Spirit and tried to reason with me.

'Son,' he said, 'it's all right if you want to speak in your prayer language in your private devotions. Just don't go around broadcasting your experience and telling other people how to receive it.'

My eyes brimmed with tears as I quietly replied, 'I can't do that, sir.'

His jaw tightened and his careful, deliberate words cut my heart like a knife. 'Then in that case, Larry, you have no ministry.'

That professor wasn't the only one concerned about my baptism in the Holy Spirit. When my father learned of my new experience, he warned, 'Larry, you're gonna wind up out under a tent somewhere with a bunch of snaggle-toothed people who foam at the mouth.'

For a while, it looked as if he might be right.

But 1972 was a big year for me: I graduated from college; I married my wife, Melva Jo; and Howard Conatser, pastor of Beverly Hills Baptist Church in Dallas, surprised me with a generous invitation to become his youth minister.

I appreciated his offer, but I really didn't want to be a youth minister. My desire was to become an evangelist like TV evangelist James Robison, and I told Pastor Conatser so.

He wasn't upset in the least. 'Just pray about it, Larry,' his raspy bass voice drawled confidently.

So I prayed, and to my astonishment, the Lord directed me to accept the position.

Back then I wasn't one to beat around the bush when a head-on confrontation would do just as well. When I learned that the youth group at Beverly Hills existed on a steady diet of skating parties, barbecues, bad-taste parties and trips to the amusement park, I strolled in before the critical stares of fifty pairs of young eyes and announced, 'Y'all, we're not gonna do all that stuff anymore. We're gonna read the red and pray for the power.'

The response was tremendous. Overnight the youth group went from fifty to fourteen. Phenomenal growth!

And to top it all, a girl sauntered up to me with a smirk on her face and fire in her eyes and threatened, 'Listen, if you don't do what we want you to do, we're gonna run you off just like we ran off the four youth directors before you!'

I sucked in my breath, commanded my little ol' insides to stop shaking, prayed she wouldn't notice the quiver in my voice and offered her an option.

'Sister,' I said as I stared her right in the eye, 'you can't run me off, because you didn't run me in. I'm here because God told me to be here, and I'm not leaving. It'll be a lot easier for you to move your membership to another church than for me to move my furniture!'

That was the end of that conversation and the beginning of a new day for many young people.

That group of fourteen began meeting on Tuesday, Wednesday, Thursday and Sunday nights. By the end of the first summer, we had grown from fourteen to a hundred and forty. By the end of the second year, we had a thousand teenagers in our youth services, and many more flocked to the Christian concerts we sponsored. God honoured my obedience to his call and the zealous witness of those young people. (Many of those same people are now members of Church on the Rock.)

But one of the most dangerous things that can befall any minister happened to me. I became a successful preacher without developing my own personal prayer life. Don't get me wrong; I sometimes prayed fervent, earnest prayers, but my prayer life was sporadic and inconsistent.

Outside, everything looked great. I preached to crowds of kids every month. We had a concert ministry which drew thousands of teenagers weekly and was telecast nationally for five years. But something was happening on the inside of me. My own preaching was convicting me. Again and again after ministering to a congregation, I found myself alone in a back room of the church, crying out to God and repenting over my prayerless life.

Those were some of the most miserable days in my memory. But God was getting ready to give me a chance to obey another call — the highest call of all.

4

The highest call of all

After Howard Conatser died in 1978, I was called to be the pastor of his three-thousand-member church. That was a very tempting offer to a twenty-eight-year-old youth minister, but right away God let me know that it wasn't for me.

A man on the committee approached me with an offer that went something like this: 'Son, we're gonna triple your salary, put you on television and make you rich and famous. You just preach sermons that bring people down the aisle and play your cards right, and we'll make you a success.'

This was another of those heart-to-heart, eye-to-eye conversations that I was becoming accustomed to, so I squared my shoulders and replied forthrightly, 'Sir, I quit playing cards when I got saved.'

Well, that bought me a ticket back home to Kilgore.

Although I was graduating from Bible college and my wife and I had three small children by this time, I moved back into the same bedroom I had slept in as a teenager in high school. My future seemed to have fallen into one glorious heap. God knows how to motivate us to pray, doesn't he!

At about that time I met Bob Willhite, pastor of the First Assembly of God Church in Kilgore, Texas, and he invited me to hold a mission in his church. Something about this soft-spoken, grey-haired gentleman captured my attention. I knew immediately that this man was to be my pastor, and I told him so.

I conducted the mission for him and his praying people. It lasted seven weeks, and we saw five hundred teenagers saved. We witnessed the conversion of the entire senior class of one of the local high schools. But the greatest thing that happened during the revival was my personal conversion from being a preacher in the pulpit to becoming a man who was more interested in prayer than anything else in life.

It came about like this. One evening I remarked, 'Pastor Willhite, I understand you're a man of prayer.'

'That's right,' he said. 'I pray. I've been rising early in the morning to pray for over thirty years.'

My pulse quickened and I said to myself, 'Oh, Jesus, this is a real one.'

Masking my excitement I asked, 'While the mission is going on, would you let me come and pray with you in the mornings?'

'Why, yes,' Pastor Willhite agreed. 'I'll pick you up in the morning at five.'

I might as well confess that when four-fifteen rolled around the next morning and that screeching alarm-clock went off, I didn't feel one ounce of anointing to pray. No angel stood by my side and commanded, 'Come, my son. Let us journey to the place of prayer.' All I wanted to do was pull the covers over my head. But I managed to stagger to the shower and to be clothed and in my right mind when Pastor Willhite's car pulled into the driveway.

As we rode to the church that morning before dawn, I didn't have any idea what God was going to do in my life, but I was absolutely certain that I was answering the most vital call of my ministry — the call to pray.

That call will haunt each of us until we answer it. It had haunted me for six years. But when I obeyed it, that choice marked the turning-point in my ministry. From that day on, I rose early every morning to pray. Of course, I sought God's *hand,* praying, 'Lord, do this for me. Do that for me.' But more and more I also found myself seeking God's *face,* thirsting for his friendship and communion, hungering for his holy, loving, compassionate nature to be formed within me.

I felt like a little child who didn't know my right hand from my left. I knew there was so very much to learn about prayer and communion with my Father. The cry of my heart became: 'Teach me how to pray, Father. Teach me how to pray.'

And one morning during that two-year period of travelling as an evangelist, while I was in prayer, the Holy Spirit began to reveal truths about the Lord's Prayer that I want to share with you later in this book.

I was in Canada conducting a youth mission when the Lord impressed upon me, 'Go to Rockwall and establish my people there.' Rockwall, a town with a population just under eleven thousand people, is perched on a ridge overlooking Lake Ray Hubbard, some twenty-five miles east of Dallas. It is a small town in the smallest county in Texas.

If God had commanded, 'Fall off the face of the earth,' I don't think I could have been any more astonished. Actually, at the time, the two orders would have appeared to be somewhat synonymous.

But I moved my family to Rockwall and began to apply the principles God had taught me about growing a church. We began Church on the Rock (COTR) in 1980 with thirteen people. We rapidly outgrew the house where we met and moved to the Rockwall Skating Rink, where we had about two hundred people on our first Sunday.

We soon overflowed that facility, so the church began holding services in the Rockwall High School cafeteria. Growing rapidly, we knew we desperately needed our own building, so we began saving every dollar we could.

One day P.J. Titus, a native of India and a long-time friend with a proven ministry, walked into my office with an urgent need. The Lord had placed upon his heart a burden to begin a Bible college in India, and it would take twenty thousand dollars to accomplish that task.

My thoughts went immediately to the twenty thousand dollars in the church's savings account that was designated for our new building, and a struggle began within me. Knowing I had something critical to pray about, I asked Titus if he could return the next day for my decision.

As we sought the Lord's will, the Holy Spirit directed us to sow, not save, our last seed. But I was not prepared for Titus's reaction. The next day when he returned to my office and I handed him a cheque for twenty thousand dollars, he burst into tears, the sobs shaking his small frame.

When he was able to speak, he told me why the cheque meant so much to him. 'I told the Lord that if you would give me the twenty thousand dollars to begin the Bible college, I would leave the United States where I've lived these past few years, return to India and spend the remainder of my life ministering to my people.'

Titus is now doing just that. Because we dared to sow our precious seed instead of eating it or hoarding it for ourselves, the Lord has given Church on the Rock the second largest Bible college in all of India, and Titus is training men and women to reach their nation for God.

But when he walked out of my office with our last twenty thousand dollars in his hand, I didn't know how it would turn out. We were still having church meetings in a rented cafeteria, and now we were back to zero financially. I believed that God would provide, but I wasn't quite prepared for the instrument he chose to work through!

One Sunday after the meeting, an honest-to-goodness Texan cowboy sidled up to me and drawled, 'You're either straight out of heaven or straight out of hell. I don't like preachers, but I like you. God told me you are to be my pastor.'

Then he took me out to his truck where he thrust an old work-boot into my hands. Seeing the bewilderment on my face, he explained, 'I've been a Christian for a long time, but being on the rodeo circuit for the last couple of years has kept me from having a church home. I've just been puttin' my tithes into this old boot. Now God says I should give it to you.'

There was over a thousand dollars inside that boot. When I peered inside, the Lord immediately nudged me that he was going to use the incident for his glory.

Taking the boot to the next service, I shared with the congregation what had happened. Spontaneously, they began to stream forward and stuff into the boot money to construct the building we needed so desperately. Sunday after Sunday, the miracle continued.

The building was finished without borrowing any money for its construction: we moved in debt-free.

Because the crowds overflowed the new auditorium the first Sunday we gathered there, we immediately increased to two Sunday services — then three, four, five — to accommodate the people. We also had to add Tuesday and Thursday night midweek services because the Wednesday evening service could not hold the crowds.

Our records reveal that the church has grown from thirteen people to over seven thousand members with a thirty-two-member pastoral staff and more than four hundred and sixty home cell-groups. To house the phenomenal harvest, it became necessary to construct a church building that would accommodate eleven thousand people.

And if all of this were not enough to thrill the heart of any thirty-six-year-old pastor, in the spring of 1986, Oral Roberts asked me to become the vice president of Oral Roberts University (ORU) and serve as dean of theological and spiritual affairs. When I protested that I could not leave my church, that sixty-eight-year-old American Indian leaned forward and said, 'I don't want you to leave your church. I want you to bring the spirit and life-flow of your church into ORU.'

My elders freed me from the administrative and counselling duties which can consume a pastor's time and released me to pray, preach in our church, direct the national prayer revival which God has called me to lead and, until recently, prepare spiritual leadership through ORU.

Have you ever stopped to reflect upon the magnitude of a simple, yet life-changing choice you made years before? I think about my choice often, and I always thank God that I answered the call that is higher than my call to preach — the call to pray.

Every believer may not be called to preach, but every Christian is called to pray. Prayer is our duty. Prayer is our privilege. Prayer, like air, water and food, is necessary for our survival and growth. But many believers regard prayer as an optional activity.

Corrie ten Boom, the beloved author of *The Hiding Place*, sometimes posed this question to believers: 'Is prayer your *spare tyre* or your *steering-wheel?*'

Meditate on that question in the privacy of your own heart and remember: There is a higher call — the call to pray. Have you answered it?

5

A divine progression

People heard God's voice yesterday, and that was good. But it is also essential that we hear his voice today. 'Today, if you hear his voice . . .' (Hebrews 3:7).

Today the Holy Spirit is speaking a word to the church. God is calling his church to pray, and we had better listen because the bottom line on all that will take place from now on is: '"Not by might nor by power, but by my Spirit," says the Lord Almighty' (Zechariah 4:6).

It is important for us to understand that the desire to pray is not something we can work up in our flesh; rather, the desire to pray is birthed in us by the Holy Spirit. If he has already implanted that divine desire in your heart, pause right now and thank God for it. If not, ask him to put it there. Then pray that God will help you transform that divine desire into daily discipline. As the discipline to pray is formed within you, discipline will 'change gears'. Prayer will no longer be duty or drudgery. It will become a holy delight.

God longs to see your heart transformed into a house of prayer. Why? Because there is so much he longs to do for you and through you. Therefore, as you begin to pray, a divine progression will take place within you. Let me explain what I mean.

It was a normal business-as-usual day in the temple at Jerusalem until the moment Jesus walked in. His grief joined hands with holy anger. After fashioning a whip from small cords, Jesus strode purposefully towards the money-changers and the buyers and sellers of oxen, sheep and doves, forcefully driving them and their mooing, cooing, bleating wares out of the temple.

Before the amazed onlookers could react, Jesus was back, this time to overthrow the tables and seats of the money-changers and dove-sellers. The scattered coins still spun and rolled across the floor as he thundered, '"My house will be called a house of prayer," but you are making it a "den of robbers"' (Matthew 21:13).

Aware that only the guilty had anything to fear, the blind and lame thronged to him in the temple, and he healed them there amid the laughter and happy hosannas of children. When the chief priests and scribes angrily demanded that Jesus quiet the children's joyful cries, he calmly countered, 'Have you never read, "From the lips of children and infants you have ordained praise"?' (see Matthew 21:12-16).

Take a moment to observe the beautiful progression in these verses. First, Jesus cleansed the temple, causing it to become a house of *purity* (v12). Then he pronounced that it would be called a house of *prayer* (v13). Next the temple was transformed into a house of *power* as the blind and the lame came to him and he healed them there (v14). And finally, the temple became a house of *perfected praise* (v16).

Shouldn't this same progression take place in the church and in the individual believer today? To echo the words of Paul, 'Don't you know that you yourselves are God's temple and that God's Spirit lives in you?' (1 Corinthians 3:16). You and I are part of the church that is the habitation of God through the Spirit (Ephesians 2:20-22). But sadly, our temples, too, are often polluted by grasping greed, manoeuvring motives and selfish sins.

It is a mockery for believers to talk one way and live another. God will not bless an impure church. His church will not become the house of power and perfected praise until it allows the Holy Spirit to purify its sanctimonious soul and transform it into a house of prayer.

Listen to God's solemn warning to his church: 'Today, if you hear his voice, do not harden your hearts as you did in the rebellion, during the time of testing in the desert' (Hebrews 3:7-8). These verses indicate that because the children of Israel heard but did not heed, their mission to possess the land of Canaan was thwarted.

God had promised that land to the children of Israel. But when ten out of twelve men sent by Moses to spy out the land returned fearful and faint-hearted because the land seemed unconquerable, an entire generation died in the wilderness. Although two of the spies, Joshua and Caleb, confidently affirmed, 'We should go up and take possession of the land, for we can certainly do it' (Numbers 13:30), when the vote was in, the tens had it over the twos.

God does not operate on our timetables. He was ready to march them across the Jordan River, but the people were caught up in petty daily routines.

A self-seeking leader remarked smugly, 'Have you noticed? Moses just isn't anointed anymore.'

A dissatisfied wife nagged her weary husband, 'You've got to get more manna for our kids!'

A well-meaning elder warned, 'Joshua and Caleb are off on a "hyper-faith" tangent. How can they run around proclaiming, "We're able to overcome," when everybody knows that the enemy is stronger than we are?'

They feared the giants instead of God. They focused on the problems instead of the promises. They saw walled cities instead of the will of God. And because they missed what the Spirit was saying, they wandered in the desert forty years. They died there and their bones bleached in the wilderness.

It's no different today. We're here to possess the

land, my friend, but instead we're busy redecorating the house, watching Saturday night football, trying to pay the mortgage and worrying about our 'stuff'. All the while, the interceding Holy Spirit is calling us to pray, and we aren't listening.

The contemporary church is far from biblical Christianity. Mediocrity has invaded the body of Christ, and we think it's normal. God is accelerating everything in these last days, yet ninety-nine per cent of us are lagging behind. We long to see God's power, but before the power of God can be revealed, we must develop the discipline of prayer.

I don't know if you have ever uttered a prayer like this, but I have: 'God, I want you to take everything out of my life that's not like Jesus. I don't want anything in me except that which glorifies and magnifies Jesus Christ the Lord.'

In order for that prayer to become a reality, things that *can* be shaken *must* be shaken so that 'what cannot be shaken may remain' (Hebrews 12:27).

After I shared that thought in a sermon, a teenager remarked, 'Sounds to me like you're talking about a whole lot of shaking goin' on.'

The girl was right. There is going to be a lot of shaking.

If you could talk to me right now, would you confide, 'Larry, a whole lot of shaking has gone on in my life these last few years'? Some of you might say the same thing about the churches you've attended. A lot of stirring, a lot of shaking, a lot of changes have taken place. Why? In order that we can take the next step in this divine progression.

Today if you hear his voice calling you to pray, don't harden your heart. Ask the Holy Spirit to give you no rest until your prayer life moves from mere desire to daily discipline and on to holy delight. Let Jesus drive out and overturn the things in your life that are preventing your temple from becoming a house of prayer. Smelly oxen, bleating sheep, cooing doves and tarnished coins are poor substitutes for the satisfying, holy presence of God.

Face the facts. If you do not begin to pray, you will not be any further along with the Lord next year than you are right now. There is always the agony of choice before the promise of change. So what will it be: business as usual or are you ready to take your next step with God?

Jesus is waiting for you to pray, 'Lord, make my temple a house of purity, prayer, power and perfected praise for your glory.'

He is ready to begin that divine progression in your temple right now. Are you?

6

Lord, teach us to pray

After his father's funeral, my friend Bob Tyndall thumbed through the worn Bible that had been one of his dad's closest companions. His glance fell upon this handwritten notation in the margin: 'Jesus didn't teach us how to preach. He didn't teach us how to sing. He taught us how to pray.'

Robert Tyndall Sr was right. Prayer was a priority with Jesus. Regarding the beginning of Christ's ministry, the Gospel of Mark says, 'Very early in the morning, while it was still dark, Jesus got up, left the house and went off to a solitary place, where he prayed' (1:35). Regarding the middle of Jesus' ministry, after he miraculously fed the five thousand, Matthew 14:23 says that Jesus went up alone into a mountain to pray. Regarding the end of Jesus' earthly ministry, Luke tells us Jesus went out, as was his habit, to pray (Luke 22:39-41).

Jesus made a habit of prayer, and he taught others to pray by his words and example. In the gospels we discover that the most exacting work Jesus did was to pray; then, overflowing with anointing and compassion, he went from those places of intercession to receive the fruits of the battles he had won in prayer — mighty miracles, authoritative revelations, wonderful healings and powerful deliverances.

Because prayer was a fixed habit of his life, it is not surprising that, even as he faced the jeers and curses from scoffers at the foot of his cross, the first words he uttered as he hung there were a prayer (Luke 23:34).

Jesus faced death as he had faced life: unafraid. As he died, he committed his spirit into his Father's keeping and said, 'It is finished' (John 19:30).

But we must not think that Christ's death marked the end of his prayer ministry. The writer to the Hebrews says that Jesus' ministry in heaven today is intercession: 'He is able to save completely those who come to God through him, because he always lives to intercede for them' (Hebrews 7:25). Jesus' continuing ministry in heaven is prayer. I am on his prayer list, and so are you.

Jesus would never do anything that was worthless or dry or dull, and he would never ask you to, either. Right now he is extending to you the highest call of all. He is repeating to you what he said to his disciples in the Garden of Gethsemane: 'Could you men not keep watch with me for one hour? . . . . Watch and pray so that you will not fall into temptation. The spirit is willing, but the body is weak' (Matthew 26:40-41). Jesus wants you to learn how to spend time with him, how to tarry with him one hour in prayer.

I think I know how you feel. I had said yes to him so many times. I had the desire, but not the discipline.

I remember an evening when I preached at a place called the Bronco Bowl in South Dallas. (That's the bowling-alley where Beverly Hills Baptist Church met after we outgrew our church building.) Three thousand teenagers were in the auditorium that night, and when I gave the invitation we saw five hundred come forward for salvation.

I'll never forget it. As I stood before that sea of earnest faces and commanded, 'Get right with God,' something inside me asked, 'When are *you* going to get right with God?' As I left the platform, others thought I was slipping away to talk to the converts, but I was actually going into a back room to lie on my face before the Lord.

I was frustrated about this matter of prayer. Looking

back, I believe it was *holy* frustration. The Spirit of God simply would not let me settle for anything else than the ministry of prayer.

I don't want to leave the wrong impression. We prayed at Beverly Hills. Sometimes we prayed all night. We prayed in a great harvest. The church grew from four hundred to well over three thousand in four years! But God was asking me to make a practice of rising early in the morning, praying through to the place of victory and walking in the authority and anointing of God. I needed a day-by-day walk — not a frantic race to get 'prayed up' for some special event.

During those days when I was minister of youth at Beverly Hills, I was invited to hold a youth mission in Hereford, Texas. Ever since my conversion, I had longed to be an evangelist; I was delighted by their invitation to come. All but one denomination in town was co-operating so each service was to be held in a different church.

The mission didn't start off too well. That first night, we went to the Church of God. It was cold outside, and it was cold inside, too. I preached as well as I could and gave the invitation, but nobody came forward for salvation.

The next night we went to the Assemblies of God church. We had a good praise and worship service, but the preaching and call for salvation were a repeat performance of the night before. I felt as if everybody was wondering, 'When's he going to do something? When's it going to happen?' That's certainly what I was thinking.

The third night we went to the Methodist church. I made sure I arrived a little early so I could get alone with God. Just as I was looking for a place to pray, two Catholic nuns with a guitar walked through the back door. They made a beeline for me and asked, 'Brother Lea, would you tune our guitar for us?'

Startled by the strange request, I just stared at them

and said, 'Well — I — er — yes, I will.' (How do you say no to two Catholic nuns?) So we slipped away to a side room where I tuned the guitar.

Sensing my nervousness as my preparation time before the service slipped away, one of the nuns put her hand on my arm and said reassuringly, 'Don't worry, Brother Lea. We've prayed for you today for eight hours.'

I could hardly believe what she had said, but nevertheless felt grateful, even relieved. She laid her hands on me and began to speak in tongues. The other one began singing in tongues. Within a few seconds I didn't know if I was terrestrial or celestial, but I knew I was with two women who really knew God!

When they had finished, one of them said to me, 'Does the phrase "It is finished" mean anything to you, Brother Lea?'

Chills went all over my body, because that was my text for the evening.

The service began, and I preached from one of those right-handed Methodist pulpits way up high in the air. At the end of the sermon I gave the invitation, and a hundred young people walked forward!

The next night I was to preach at the Catholic church. I got there early and breathed a sigh of relief when I saw the two nuns walk in the back door carrying their guitar. This time I ran right up to them and asked, 'Could I tune your guitar for you?' My heart hadn't been in it the night before but it really was this time.

We went through the little guitar-tuning ritual, and I got down to business. Without batting an eyelid, I said, 'Let's do it again; you know, what we did last night.'

So they laid their hands on me, and it happened again. Then the nun who had never spoken a word of English in my presence asked casually, 'Brother Lea, you remember the woman who had the issue of blood and reached out to touch the hem of Jesus' garment?' (You guessed it. That was the text I had chosen for my sermon that evening!)

I preached, and a hundred more people found God that night. By the end of the week, five hundred people had been saved in that small town.

As I flew back to Dallas, I tried to figure out just exactly how, in my most humble way, I would announce at the staff meeting what God had done through me. 'How did the youth mission go?' 'Oh, not too bad — we had five hundred saved. It was a pretty good week.'

I had always wanted to be an evangelist. Now I *knew* I was an evangelist, and it felt wonderful. I was gloating over the number of people saved, thinking about how I could report it meekly, when the Holy Spirit abruptly interrupted my musings.

'Son,' he said, 'let's get one thing straight. You had nothing at all to do with that mission.'

My mouth dropped open, but I shut it fast.

The voice inside me continued: 'What happened was simply that somebody *prayed the price.'*

Those words rang in my ears for years afterwards. Prayed the price! Somebody prayed the price.

By 1978 when Pastor Conatser passed away and I was extended the call to become the pastor of Beverly Hills Baptist Church, my holy frustration had reached a climax. I was at the place where nothing mattered anymore except the call to pray. I had to answer this call, this call which was higher than the call to preach. That's when I took my little family and went back home to Kilgore, Texas. That's when I met B.J. Willhite and my desperate *desire* to prayer shifted into holy *discipline*.

It was during those days, while I searched for wisdom as a person would search for lost money or hidden treasure, that the Lord began to reveal to me new things, hidden things about prayer that I had not known before. As I continually cried out to him, he poured revelation into my spirit.

By the time he commanded me to go to Rockwall and establish his people there, I had been delivered from the theology that says, 'Big is better.' I went to Rockwall with one thought in mind, and that was to equip some people and teach them how to pray. I did not know I was moving right into the taproot of the very thing that blossomed into the outpouring of the power of God in the first century. I just knew I had to pray and I had to teach other people how to pray.

Our church was about a year old in 1981 when I went to New Orleans to hear Paul Yonggi Cho, pastor of Yoido Full Gospel Church in Seoul, Korea, the largest church in the world. The Lord helped me get in to see him, and we met in a small back room of the church hosting the seminar. As my eyes met his, I felt as if I were looking right into the man's soul.

I knew we had only a minute and my one-liner had better be good, so I blurted out something like, 'Dr Cho, how did you build such a great church?'

He smiled back at me and, with no hesitation, replied, 'I pray, and I obey.' And then he laughed.

I chuckled with him, but inside I was rehearsing his words. 'That's the key,' I muttered to myself. 'That's it right there. Pray and obey, Larry. Pray and obey.'

I will never forget his words. You see, there are a lot of people who want to obey, but they don't pray. And there are some people who pray, but don't have the courage to obey. But prayer and obedience must go hand in hand if we are to move into the power and anointing of the Spirit of God.

I'm convinced that the disciples weren't much different from you and me. Like us, they had to beat their brains out against one brick wall after another before they came to Jesus and said, 'Lord, teach us to pray.'

That's the way it was for me. I tried to pray on my

own, but I knew there was something missing. I kept crying out to God, 'Lord, teach me how to pray. Teach me how to pray.' And one day, no sooner were those words out of my mouth, than the lessons began.

7

Could you not tarry one hour?

When I asked the Lord to teach me how to tarry with him an hour in prayer, I remembered that Jesus instructed his disciples, 'This . . . is how you should pray' (Matthew 6:9). I opened my Bible to the verses we have come to call 'the Lord's Prayer' and pondered those sixty-six words:

'Our Father in heaven, hallowed be your name, your kingdom come, your will be done on earth as it is in heaven. Give us today our daily bread. Forgive us our debts, as we also have forgiven our debtors. And lead us not into temptation, but deliver us from the evil one, for yours is the kingdom and the power and the glory for ever. Amen. (Matthew 6:9-13 margin).

I was puzzled, and I said so. 'Lord, I can say that in twenty-two seconds, and I can sing it in a minute and a half. How is this ever going to help me tarry with you an hour?'

The Spirit of God answered: 'Say it really slowly.'

Like an obedient child, I began reciting the familiar words, pausing after each short phrase: 'Our Father in heaven . . . hallowed be your name . . . .' Just as those words were out of my mouth, the Spirit of God began to drop into my heart a series of revelations and visions that planted me once and for all in the discipline of prayer and shifted my prayer life into holy delight.

I hope it doesn't upset anybody when I admit that I saw a vision. I can almost see the eyebrows going up. Do you know what's wrong with believers today? We've studied the counterfeit for so long, we don't even recognise the original anymore. It's a shame that a boy who had attended church off and on for seventeen years wound up in a psychiatric ward before he found out God could talk!

If only I had known someone like those two little Catholic nuns I told you about. One of them came up to me some time ago and asked with a smile, 'Do you know how I know things?'

I returned her grin and asked, 'How?'

She replied matter-of-factly, 'I know 'em in my "knower"!'

If you are a believer, you, too, have a 'knower'. It is the witness of the Holy Spirit.

After I asked the question, 'Lord, how can I learn to tarry with you one hour?' the Lord made me a promise.

'When you learn to tarry with me one hour,' he pledged, 'something supernatural will happen in your life.' And then he showed me that what we call 'the Lord's Prayer' is actually a prayer outline.

You see, the first-century rabbis usually taught by giving topics of truth. They listed certain topics and then, under each topic, the rabbis provided a complete outline. In his model prayer, Jesus enumerated topics and instructed: 'This . . . is how you should pray' (Matthew 6:9-13). We have memorised, quoted and sung the Lord's Prayer, but we have not seen it as a group of six topics to be followed in prayer under the guidance of the Holy Spirit.

My friend Brad Young, author of *The Jewish Background to the Lord's Prayer,* says that certain ancient writings contain prayers of early Christians which are based upon the Lord's Prayer and require about one hour to pray through.

Young also made a fascinating observation based on Acts 1:14. You remember that the disciples, along with Mary the mother of Jesus, Christ's brothers and other believers, gathered in the upper room after Jesus' ascension, in obedience to his command to wait for the Holy Spirit? Scripture records: 'They all joined together constantly in prayer.' Young pointed out that the Greek does not read 'in prayer'; rather, this verse actually states: 'They all joined together constantly in "the Prayer".' He said that ancient literature often refers to the Lord's Prayer as 'the Prayer'.

Today a new generation of disciples is discovering the principles, purpose and power behind the familiar words of the Lord's Prayer. And, as we rediscover the power and necessity of prayer, our prayer lives are moving from desire to discipline to delight.

As you discipline yourself to take this prayer outline and come into God's presence, prayer will become your life flow as it was the life flow of Jesus and the early church. But I should sound this warning: This is no little ten-watt truth; it's a powerful two-hundred-and-forty-watt revelation that can illuminate your temple with the glory of God and transform your house of prayer into a house of power and perfected praise.

If you're ready, plug in.

Part Two

Promises

*'Our Father in heaven,
hallowed be your name'*

8

Appropriating God's names

Discipline is a dirty word to many of us. When most people think about discipline in prayer, they get a grim, determined look on their faces, grit their teeth and vow, 'I'm going to do it if it kills me!'

That's the look my young son, John Aaron, put on his face when I told him to eat his spinach. 'Daddy,' he said in his most man-to-man voice, 'I don't *like* it, but I can *eat* it.'

How many times have you said that to God: 'Father, I don't *like* to pray, but I can *do* it'? Prayer doesn't have to be a duty; it can be a delight.

Have you ever noticed that the Lord's Prayer begins and ends with praise? We are to enter his gates with thanksgiving and his courts with praise (Psalm 100:4). Jesus knew this when he instructed, 'When you pray, say: Our Father in heaven, hallowed be your name' (Luke 11:2 margin).

Love says 'our' and faith says 'Father'. The omniscient, omnipotent Creator-God dwelling in eternity invites believers to call him Father.

The word 'hallow' is not a common word, but it means 'to sanctify or set apart; to praise; to adore'. The phrase should be translated, 'May your name be sanctified.' It is the expression of an intense desire that God's name be recognised, set apart and adored.

We don't stop to realise that the name of the Lord can be either sanctified or profaned by our conduct. But ancient documents record that, because a martyr's sacrificial death would frequently cause others to glorify God, the Hebrew idiom 'to sanctify the name'

was often understood to mean to give one's life for his
faith.[1]

What a powerful truth! We can sanctify God by the
example of our righteous lives, as well as by our words
of praise and adoration (Matthew 5:16).

As we learn to follow Christ's prayer pattern and
to set apart, praise and adore the name of God, prayer
will shift out of frustrating desire and determined
discipline and move right on into holy delight.

The discipline I am talking about will lead you into
God's holy presence and cause you to walk in kingdom
priorities. It will help you learn how to 'pray in' what
you need and will enable you to get along with
everybody all the time. It will help you face the devil
and leave him sitting in the dirt. It will cause you to
be the head and not the tail, to be above only and not
beneath. It will enable you to walk in victory every
day of your life.

But in order to hallow our Father's name, we must
understand that God's character and will for his
children are revealed in his names. Our Father's
names reveal what he has promised to be *in* us and
what he has promised to do *for* and *through* us.

Blessings brought by Jesus' blood

As God was revealing the prayer outline to me he gave
me a clear vision of what God has given us. I saw Jesus
picking up a large basin and walking towards what I
perceived to be a huge rock altar behind which shone
a great light. As I watched, the Lord emptied the
contents of the basin upon the altar, and I realised that
the living, swirling liquid poured out upon that altar
was his own blood.

The Word of God flooded my mind: 'You know that
it was not with perishable things such as silver or gold
that you were redeemed from the empty way of life

[1] Brad Young, *The Jewish Background to the Lord's Prayer*, Centre for Judaic-
Christian Studies, Austin, Texas, 1984

. . . but with the precious blood of Christ, a lamb without blemish or defect' (1 Peter 1:18-19).

Suddenly it all came together: 'God sent his Son . . . to redeem those under law, that we might receive the full rights of sons. Because you are sons, God sent the Spirit of his Son into our hearts, the Spirit who calls out, "*Abba,* Father"' (Galatians 4:4-6).

I looked at that blood and exclaimed, 'Father, Father!' for into my 'knower' there came a warm and wonderful witness that, when I received Christ's forgiveness, I was adopted into the family of God and accepted as his child and heir. God was my Father by virtue of the blood of Jesus.

Then it seemed as if the living blood upon that altar spoke of the covenant blessings it had bought for me.

First, it testified that all my sins are forgiven, and I remembered, 'He was pierced for our transgressions, he was crushed for our iniquities' (Isaiah 53:5). I looked at that blood and wept both for sorrow and for joy, because I knew he had washed me from my sins in his own blood (Revelation 1:5), and sin no longer had dominion over me (Romans 6:14).

Then the blood testified that because of the blood of the Lamb, I can boldly enter into the Most Holy Place (Hebrews 10:19-20). My body has now become the temple of the Holy Spirit, who lives in me and is God's gift to me (1 Corinthians 6:19). I praised God that the blood of Jesus has opened up a new and living way in order that I might experience the fulness of the Holy Spirit.

Next, the blood testified to me that by Christ's wounds and sufferings I am healed and made whole (Isaiah 53:5; 1 Peter 2:24; Matthew 8:16-17) — healed spiritually and physically, mentally and emotionally. Jesus is the Great Physician, the sympathising Jesus.

And then the blood testified that Christ has made me free from the law of sin and death (Romans 8:2). Jesus took the curse of my failure and insufficiency

(Galatians 3:13), and now he always causes me to triumph in Christ (2 Corinthians 2:14).

Last of all, the blood testified that in my covenant relationship with God my Father, I am free from the fear of death and hell. Jesus Christ has abolished death and has brought life and immortality to light through the gospel (2 Timothy 1:10).

As the Spirit of the Lord revealed what the blood has done for us, I suddenly recalled the Hebrew names of God compounded with the name *Jehovah* in the Old Testament.

You see, when God wished to make a special revelation of himself, he used the name *Jehovah*. In that name, he revealed himself as the true and eternal God, the one who is absolutely self-existent, the one who is unchangeable.

The significance and origin of the name *Jehovah* are especially brought out in God's revelation of himself to Moses at the burning bush (Exodus 3:13-15). Through four centuries of oppression in Egypt, the children of Israel had believed in God's existence, but they had not experienced his presence. God proclaimed to Moses that he had personally come down to deliver his people from bondage and to lead them into the promised land. But before his servant Moses could lead God's people, Moses had to learn who God was and is.

When the Lord first proclaimed to Moses, 'I AM WHO I AM,' the name he used for himself was considered by Hebrew translators too sacred to be spoken aloud. So they used the consonants YHWH or JHVH, which we can read as *Yahweh* or *Jehovah*.

Yahweh implies more than just God's *existence;* it implies his personal, intimate *presence.* God's name *Jehovah* reveals his readiness to save his people and to act for them. Thus, the name *Jehovah,* or 'I AM WHO I AM', can be rendered, 'I am with you, ready to save and to act, just as I have always been.'

In the Old Testament, there are eight names compounded with the name *Jehovah: Jehovah-tsidkenu, Jehovah-m'kaddesh, Jehovah-shammah, Jehovah-shalom, Jehovah-rophe, Jehovah-jireh, Jehovah-nissi* and *Jehovah-rohi.* Each of these names is a revelation of the character and nature of God.

In Exodus 6:3-4, God links his name Jehovah to his covenant with Abraham, Isaac and Jacob. But the eight compound names of God in the Old Testament also correspond to the five-fold promise God makes to his people in the new covenant or New Testament. While God's names reveal different dimensions of his character they also point to their fulfilment in the person and work of Jesus Christ.

What are the five promises or benefits in the new covenant with which the eight compound names of God correspond? Of what five things did the testifying blood on the altar speak?

The benefits we enjoy in the new covenant deal with five vital areas. To make the areas easy to remember, I will begin each with an *s:* 1. sins — forgiveness of sins and deliverance from sin's dominion; 2. Spirit — the fulness of the Holy Spirit; 3. soundness — the promise of health and healing; 4. success — freedom from the law's curse of failure and insufficiency; 5. security — freedom from the fear of death and hell.

As the Spirit of the Lord revealed what the blood has done for us, I began to understand what it means to pray, 'Our Father in heaven, hallowed be your name.' Let's look at the five benefits given to us by virtue of Jesus' death.

Forgiveness of sins and deliverance from sin's dominion

The first benefit you enjoy in the new covenant because you are a child of God by virtue of the blood of Jesus is the *forgiveness of sins.*

How can a sinful person be acquitted of unrighteous-

ness and become righteous before God? In the Old
Testament, the penalty of death incurred because of
sin had to be borne by an innocent sufferer whose
righteousness would be reckoned to the sinner.

But no human being is innocent and righteous, and
the blood of animals cannot take away sin. Therefore,
there had to be a divine remedy. The provision of
righteousness was made in Jesus Christ, God's only
Son, who died in our place (2 Corinthians 5:21; 1 Peter
3:18).

The compound name of God, *Jehovah-tsidkenu*
(sid-kay-noo), means 'Jehovah Our Righteousness'
(see Jeremiah 23:5-6). This name reveals the facet of
God's character that transacts the redemption by
which humankind is fully restored to God.

Jesus Christ, our *Jehovah-tsidkenu,* was substituted
for us (Romans 5:17-19). The name 'Jehovah Our
Righteousness' reveals the method of our acceptance
before God ('God made him who had no sin to be sin
for us') and the measure of our acceptance ('that in
him we might become the righteousness of God') —
2 Corinthians 5:21.

Therefore as you pray, 'Hallowed be your name,
Jehovah-tsidkenu,' thank God that he has already made
a decision about your sins. In his mind he already says,
'I forgive you.' All you have to do is come and
appropriate that forgiveness, for the Bible says, 'If we
confess our sins, he is faithful and just and will forgive
us our sins and purify us from all unrighteousness' (1
John 1:9).

Do you get it? *Righteousness equals Jesus Christ
plus nothing.* 'You have been given fulness in Christ'
(Colossians 2:10). Remember the words of the old
hymn *Rock of Ages:* 'Nothing in my hand I bring, Simply
to thy cross I cling'? That's it! Let me share a story
to illustrate this profound truth.

Some years ago I was away from home preaching
in a black church. (I don't believe in reincarnation, but

I sometimes jokingly say that if I did, I'd ask to come back as a black preacher. Talk about liberty!) My dad, who was saved about two-and-a-half years before this time after having been an alcoholic for fifteen years, came to the motel where I was staying to drive me to the church.

I was eager to see him, but as I answered his knock at the door, my heart sank.

It wasn't raining, yet there he stood dripping wet. His dark hair was plastered to his scalp and his expensive blue suit and leather shoes oozed water that made puddles on the concrete balcony outside my door.

My first thought was, 'Oh, no! Dad got drunk and fell in the pool.' But I didn't want to confront him without hearing some kind of explanation. I invited him in, handed him a towel and asked very calmly, 'Dad, are you all right?'

As he mopped the water off his face, he explained what had happened.

He had been on his way to my room when he glanced down from the second storey balcony and saw the body of a small child lying motionless at the bottom of the pool. Without a second thought, he jumped off the balcony, hurdled the chain-link fence that enclosed the pool and dived into the water. He hauled the boy's limp form out of the pool, gave him artificial respiration, got him breathing and carried the frightened child to his grateful mother.

I was so proud of my dad that day. And I'll never forget that incident because that's what *Jehovah-tsidkenu*, 'the Lord Our Righteousness', did for me — and you. We were dead in the water, dead in trespasses and sins, but he jumped into the pool and saved us. He who knew no sin was made to be sin for us that we might be made the righteousness of God in him (2 Corinthians 5:21).

If you can swim your way out or buy your way out

or confess your way out, you don't need a Saviour. But if you're dead in the water, you've got to have Jesus. You must exchange your sin and guilt for his righteousness and grace if you hope to obtain eternal life.

I don't know about you, but when I remember how Jesus carried my sin and died for me on the cross, I don't have any trouble hallowing his name, *Jehovah-tsidkenu,* 'the Lord My Righteousness'.

But Jesus is more than our righteousness. He offers not only forgiveness for our sins; he offers deliverance from sin's dominion, because Jesus is our sanctifier. Now what does that mean? The primary meaning of the Hebrew word *sanctify* is 'to set apart for God's service'. Believers are to be different from, set apart from, the world by obeying God's commands.

God is holy, separate from his people, yet he sanctifies us and makes us holy in order that we might have fellowship with him. In Leviticus 20:8, he is called *Jehovah-m'kaddesh* (ma-ka-desh), 'the Lord Who Sanctifies'. But because this name has not been transliterated in our English Bibles as have his other names, it has often escaped notice as one of the compound names of Jehovah.

God's Holy Spirit indwells believers and empowers them to live holy lives and to be spiritually and morally pure (see 1 Corinthians 6:11; 1 Thessalonians 4:3-4; 5:23). Therefore, as you meditate upon God's name, 'Jehovah Who Sanctifies', praise him because the blood of Jesus not only takes away your sin; it breaks the power of sin in you. Thank him that the blood of Christ does not overlook sin; it overcomes (see Romans 6:17-18; Hebrews 13:12; 1 Corinthians 6:9-11).

Hallowed be your name, *Jehovah-m'kaddesh,* 'the Lord Who Sanctifies'.

Spirit: The fulness of the Holy Spirit

Because God is your Father, the second benefit you enjoy in the New Covenant is *the fulness of the Holy Spirit*. The compound name of God, *Jehovah-shalom* (sha-lom), means 'Jehovah is Peace' (see Judges 6:24). The Hebrew word *shalom* is most often and most appropriately translated 'peace' and represents wholeness and harmony with God and contentment and satisfaction in life.

Christ's atonement is the basis for peace with God. Before humankind could be reconciled to God, someone had to pay the price of sin, which was death. Jesus Christ paid that price, and the fellowship between God and man which sin broke was atoned for by his blood (see Colossians 1:20-22). 'The chastisement needful to obtain peace and well-being for us was upon him' (Isaiah 53:5 Amp).

As Jesus died and his blood broke down the barrier of sin separating us from God, something supernatural occurred in the Jerusalem temple. The inner veil separating the Holy Place from the Holy of Holies (God's presence chamber containing the ark and the mercy seat stained by the sacrificial animal blood which was brought in by the high priest once each year) was torn from top to bottom, opening the way for us to enter into the Holy of Holies — into the very presence of God himself (see Hebrews 10:19-22).

Josephus, a first century Pharisee and historian, reported that this four-inch-thick veil, which was renewed every year, could not be pulled apart by horses tied to each side. It barred all but the high priest from the presence of God. But when it suddenly ripped apart from top to bottom at the death of Jesus (Mark 15:37-38), access to God was made available to all who come to him through Jesus.

Hallowed be your name, *Jehovah-shalom,* 'the Lord is Peace'. Thank you for restoring humankind to that peace with God which was lost through the fall.

Another compound name of God, *Jehovah-shammah* (sham-ma), means 'Jehovah is There' (see Ezekiel 48:35). *Shammah* is the Hebrew word meaning 'the overflowing, ever-present One'. This name is the promise of a holy God dwelling in the midst of his people. It is the promise of his presence.

The presence of God himself is in believers, who are the living, growing, holy temple of God, through the Spirit (see Ephesians 2:19-22). The word used for 'temple' in verse 21 does not refer to the temple in general, but the 'sanctuary'. In the sanctuary stood the altar of incense, and in the holiest place of all was the mercy seat above which the divine presence or the Shekinah glory hovered. Now, through Jesus, we are temples of clay filled with the glorious presence of God.

Thank God that because your sins are forgiven you can be filled and flooded with God himself: you can be filled with his Holy Spirit. And that's not all. Jesus promised, 'Never will I leave you; never will I forsake you' (Hebrews 13:5). He has sent the comforting, strengthening, interceding, communing Holy Spirit to your side.

Hallowed be your name, *Jehovah-shammah*, 'the Lord is There'.

Remember, you are hallowing God's name because of who he is and because of what he has done for you. As you meditate upon the various names of God your Father, affirm your faith by turning your thoughts into declarations of faith and praise.

'Father, you are *Jehovah-tsidkenu*. You are my righteousness. I stand before you righteous and forgiven because of the blood of your dear Son.

'You are *Jehovah-m'kaddesh*, 'the Lord Who Sanctifies'. You conform me into the image of your Son and break sin's power over me.

'You are *Jehovah-shalom*, my peace. Jesus made peace by the blood of his cross and reconciled me to you. Now your peace which passes all understanding keeps my heart and my mind.

'You are *Jehovah-shammah*. You have filled me with your overflowing presence, and you will never leave me nor forsake me. Thank you for living in me, Lord.'

That is an example of what it means to hallow God's name and to make faith declarations based upon who he is and what he has done for you. But there is much more for which you should hallow your Father's name.

9

Appropriating God's promises

Don't get me wrong. Prayer is not magic, nor is it easy. But prayer works. As we acknowledge him in all our ways, God really does give us the desires of our hearts.

Some time after I became a Christian, my mother confided to me that she planned to leave my dad. 'Larry,' she sighed, 'your dad and I have lived together all these years, and it's been a terrible life. I just can't take his drinking anymore. I can't keep living this way.'

Crushed, I pleaded, 'Mum, please don't leave him.'

But Mother countered, 'You're gone now, and your sister has grown up and left home. Why shouldn't I leave?'

'Because, Mum,' I answered, 'I've been reading the red part of my Bible.'

'Well, what's that supposed to mean?' Mother asked wearily, a note of exasperation in her voice.

'It means that Jesus said in Matthew 18:19, "If two of you on earth agree about anything you ask for, it will be done for you by my Father in heaven." I'm one, Mother, and you make two. We can agree and it can be done.'

But Mother didn't share my excitement. She just took a deep breath and admitted, 'I don't even have enough faith to believe, Larry.'

'That's okay,' I said. 'It doesn't say, "If two of you agree and believe." It just says, "If two of you agree." If it takes believing, then I'll believe for both of us.'

I put my arm around her, and we prayed a prayer of agreement.

Do you know what happened after that conversation?

Things got worse! Has that ever happened to you? Did you ever pray for something really hard, but things just got worse?

One night after Dad got drunk and wrecked his car, I knelt down beside him and tried to talk to him about God, but he levelled me with the back of his hand and snarled, 'Don't tell me about that Jesus stuff!'

That night I prayed a puddle of hot tears on my bedroom floor. Jesus had kindled a burning desire in my heart for my dad's salvation, and I refused to give up. You see, I had his promise: 'Delight yourself in the Lord and he will give you the desires of your heart' (Psalm 37:4).

That doesn't mean I could have a Cadillac this week, a Mercedes next month and a new house next year. I'm not talking about carnal craziness. I'm talking about losing your life in Jesus and letting him plant his desires in your heart.

The next week I walked into the kitchen and found my mother sitting at the kitchen table crying. My first thought was that something terrible must have happened. 'Mother!' I exclaimed in alarm. 'What's happened?'

She dabbed at her tears and replied, 'I don't know exactly. All I know is that your dad pulled over by the side of the road today, got out of the car and prayed, "Jesus, if you can do anything with an old drunk like me, I'll give my life to you."'

Within the next few days, I received a call from a hospital in Dallas where my dad had been admitted because his body was totally devastated by alcohol. My father's familiar voice ordered, 'Son, bring me a Bible.'

Astonished by his request, I said, 'Dad, what's happened to you?'

Embarrassed, yet proud of his new commitment, he replied sternly, 'You *know* what's happened to me.' But his tone softened as he repeated, 'Bring me a Bible.'

With a Bible under my arm I rushed down to the

convalescent centre. As I walked into his room, Dad embraced me. The first words out of his mouth were: 'Would you pray for me?'

Together we fell on our faces and cried and prayed. That was over fifteen years ago. My dad has remained sober ever since, and he's the best friend I've ever had. He and my mother are members of my church, driving seventy miles each way every Sunday to attend services. It all happened because my faithful Lord planted a holy desire in my heart to see my dad healed and made whole in spirit, soul and body. That's the third benefit we enjoy in the new covenant: health and healing.

Soundness: Health and healing

The compound name of God, *Jehovah-rophe* (ro-phay), means 'Jehovah Heals'. The word *rophe* means 'to restore, cure or heal not only in the physical sense but also in the spiritual and moral sense'. That's what God did for my dad.

In my systematic theology class at Bible college, professors tried to tell me that Jesus doesn't heal in our day; then they attempted to convince me that this new covenant was better than the old. I didn't buy it, and neither should you! He is still 'the healer God'.

Do you or does someone you know need healing? Then begin to thank the Lord that by his stripes (or wounds) we are healed (see Isaiah 53:5; Matthew 8:16-17). Healing is already a finished work in the mind of God (1 Peter 2:24).

Make that faith declaration. Concentrate on the blood, not on yourself or how you feel. Concentrate on who he is and what his blood has purchased for you. As you praise him, he will be what you need him to be — he will be *Jehovah-rophe,* 'the Lord Who Heals'.

Put yourself in a faith position before God. Remember, the greatest faith words ever spoken are 'thank you'. Therefore, stir yourself up to give thanks for the stripes he took on his back for your healing. Hallow his name, *Jehovah-rophe,* and thank him for the health and healing that are yours through Jesus Christ.

Success: Freedom from the curse of the law

The fourth benefit you enjoy because of the covenant relationship with God your Father is *freedom from the curse of the law.*

When I was growing up, my home environment wasn't too positive. My dad used to shake his head at me in disgust and mutter, 'I'll probably have to support you for the rest of my life.'

I half believed him. I felt doomed to failure; I really didn't expect to succeed in life. The real Larry Lea never seemed to measure up to anybody's expectation.

I thought it was just me. I didn't know Paul plainly declared in Romans 3:23: 'All have sinned and fall short of the glory of God.' Our sins condemn us to failure. All men and women fall short continually in every area of life: morally, emotionally, financially, socially, spiritually and physically. No mortal has ever fulfilled all the requirements of the law.

I was preaching on this subject once when I uttered the worst preacher 'blooper' of my entire ministry. Waxing eloquent, I exclaimed, 'All have sinned and fall short of the glory of God.' Then, pointing towards the congregation, I asked, 'How many of you are tired of always falling short? Well, I've got good news for you. Christ has redeemed us from all our falling shorts.'

Christ had redeemed us, but there was no way for me to redeem that situation! My wife laughed so hard she almost fell out of her chair. But the fact of the matter is, Christ truly has redeemed us from all our 'falling shorts'.

In Galatians 3:10 we read, 'Cursed is everyone who does not continue to do everything written in the Book of the Law.' However, Romans 8:2 states, 'Through Christ Jesus the law of the Spirit of life set me free from the law of sin and death.' And in Galatians 3:13, Paul declares: 'Christ redeemed us from the curse of the law by becoming a curse for us, for it is written: "Cursed is everyone who is hung on a tree."'

What is this curse of the law from which Christ has redeemed us? To answer that question, we must return to the book of Genesis and its account of the fall of humankind.

Adam and Eve's decision to disobey God, a decision resulting in the fall of our first parents, had far-reaching effects. By their act of disobedience, sin and all its dreadful consequences entered into the world. God's image in humankind became distorted and marred, human beings became alienated from their Creator and all humankind came under a sentence of death.

Through Moses God gave men and women his law that set forth the only standard of righteousness acceptable to God. The Mosaic Law, a covenant of works, established a model for humankind's everyday conduct; however, lacking power to conform to that perfect standard, men and women always fell short. The curse of the broken law meant humanity was doomed to a frustrating, hopeless lifestyle of failure.

But when we fell into sin, we also fell into God's arms of redeeming mercy. Jesus Christ, God's only Son, and the only perfect human, voluntarily offered himself up on the cross, bore the death penalty of the curse for us, satisfied every demand of the law, and gave us a new and better covenant.

New covenant believers are free from the law's condemnation because Christ's righteousness has been imputed to them. In addition, as a result of Christ's atonement, the commandments of the law become, not impossible standards, but gracious duties and privileges willingly and effectively carried out by a redeemed people possessing the power of the Holy Spirit.

But that's not all that Jesus Christ accomplished for us when he took away our curse. Through Jesus, God's riches belong to his covenant people, riches that cover every conceivable need on this earth.

According to Galatians 3:14, Christ redeemed us from the curse of the law in order that the blessing of Abraham might come on us. What was the blessing of Abraham? Genesis 24:1 tells us that the Lord blessed Abraham in all things. Paul reasons, 'He who did not spare his own Son, but gave him up for us all — how will he not also, along with him, graciously give us all things?' (Romans 8:32).

Deuteronomy 28 details the blessings God has ordained to overtake obedient believers, blessings which are ours through Jesus Christ. Let me list some of them. God's blessings will be upon you, your family and your material possessions (v4). God will cause your enemies to be defeated (v7). The Lord will command his blessing upon your storehouse (your treasury) and upon all you undertake (v8). He will open his treasury to you in order that you might lend and not have to borrow from others (v12). You will be successful, for God will make you the head and not the tail. You will be above and not beneath (v13).

However, if God's covenant people do not obey him and walk in his ways, God promises to rebuke every enterprise to which they set their hands and to allow them to be overtaken by curses, confusion, poverty, failure and devastating diseases (Deuteronomy 28: 15-45).

Thus Jesus, as we have seen, took the curse of our failure and insufficiency and became our source of success and blessing, our *Jehovah-jireh* (pronounced 'yeer-a' in Hebrew, but commonly pronounced 'ji-ra'). The name *Jehovah-jireh* means 'the Lord Who Sees' or 'Jehovah's Provision Shall be Seen' (see Genesis 22, especially v14).

God our Father sees our needs beforehand and makes provision for them. His name, *Jehovah-jireh,* is a revelation of God's willingness and ability to make provision for our sin and need. Because Jesus has taken the curse away, we are free from moral, financial, emotional, social or spiritual failure, for God has *ordained* our success. We can do all things through Christ (see Philippians 4:13).

Therefore, as you hallow his name, *Jehovah-jireh,* thank God that you are free from the curse. Make the praise declaration that Jesus, who was made a curse for you, has freed you, and you do not have to live under the curse of the law. The writer of an old hymn made such a declaration: 'Though earth hinders and hell rages, all must work for good to thee.'

Sing it! Say it! Believe it!

Security: Freedom from the fear of death and hell

The fifth benefit you enjoy in your covenant relationship with God your Father is *freedom from the fear of death and hell.*

The compound name of God, *Jehovah-nissi* (nis-see), means 'Jehovah My Banner' (see Exodus 17:15). The word for *banner* might also be translated 'pole, ensign or standard'. Among the Jews, it is also a word denoting 'miracle'. As an ensign or standard, it was a rallying-point to kindle hope and efforts, a signal raised on an elevated place on a special occasion. The banner represented God's cause, his battle, and was a sign of deliverance and salvation.

Isaiah predicted that a rod would come forth out of the stem of Jesse which would be an *ensign* (flag or banner) of the people (Isaiah 11:10). That stem of Jesse is Jesus Christ (Romans 1:3). Jesus, our banner of redemption and warfare, was lifted up on a rugged cross on Mount Calvary. He has gone before us and conquered the world and its power to harm us (John 16:33 Amp).

God has exalted Christ far above all other rulers, authorities and powers, put all things under his feet and appointed him the head of the church (Ephesians 1:18-23). Now Jesus goes into battle before believers, gives us the victory and makes us conquerors (1 Corinthians 15:57).

When Jesus Christ, our banner, was resurrected from the dead, he abolished death and brought life and immortality to light through the gospel (see 2 Timothy 1:10). Now we no longer have to fear death, for Jesus Christ's death and resurrection rendered powerless him who had the power of death, Satan (Hebrews 2:14-15). Christ's banner over us is love, and love never fails.

Another compound name of God, *Jehovah-rohi* (ro-ee), means 'Jehovah My Shepherd' (see Psalm 23). The primary meaning of *rohi* or *ro'eh* is 'to feed or lead to pasture, as a shepherd does his flock'. It can also be translated 'companion' or 'friend'.

Jesus is the shepherd of his people (John 10:11; Hebrews 13:20), and he feeds, leads, protects and cares for his sheep. Because he is our shepherd, we do not have to fear death (see Psalm 23:1, 4, 6; 1 Corinthians 15:55-57).

As you meditate upon the cross, praise the Lord that you are free from death and hell because your sin was taken away at Calvary. Praise him because you will never perish, but will have eternal life. Focus on Jesus who was crucified and declare: 'I have been crucified with Christ and I no longer live, but Christ lives in me' (Galatians 2:20).

Consider this: If you are a believer, and someone took a gun and shot you right now, your earthly body would slump in death, but your living spirit would go immediately into the presence of the Lord (see 2 Corinthians 5:8). Once your spirit grasps the truth that you are an eternal creature who will never die, you will live differently, talk differently, walk differently.

You are an eternal being, already experiencing eternal life.

Thank God that he is your banner who has conquered death, hell and the grave. Praise the Lord because he is your shepherd who will lead you through the valley of the shadow of death and into the house of the Lord, where you will dwell for ever.

Hallowed be your name, *Jehovah-nissi,* 'the Lord My Banner'. Hallowed be your name, *Jehovah-rohi,* 'the Lord My Shepherd'.

Philippians 2:9-10 says: 'God exalted him to the highest place and gave him the name that is above every name, that at the name of Jesus every knee should bow.' The knees of every foe must bow and acknowledge Christ's supreme authority, power and dominion. The full character and nature of God the Father are found in the name of Jesus. The *Jehovah* names of God apply to Jesus, who said, 'I have come in my Father's name' (John 5:43). 'In Christ all the fulness of the Deity lives in bodily form,' states Paul in Colossians 2:9.

By believing on Jesus' name we are born again (John 1:12-13), and by believing on his name we live in victory. We must submit to the lordship of Jesus and to the dominion of that name in every area of our lives, for Paul said, 'Everyone who confesses the name of the Lord must turn away from wickedness' (2 Timothy 2:19).

If we allow anything in our lives that is not his nature and will, we are misusing his name. We are not sanctifying his name; we are profaning it. Therefore, we must submit to the lordship of Jesus and to the dominion of his name in every area of our lives, for God has commanded, 'You shall not misuse the name of the Lord your God' (Exodus 20:7).

In the great Azusa Street revival of the early 1900s, this altar invitation was given: 'Everyone interested in pardon, sanctification, healing and the baptism in the Holy Spirit, rise and come.' The speaker was right. Jesus is our righteousness, sanctifier, peace, healer, provider, banner and shepherd, and he is the overflowing one present within us.

Our Father in heaven, hallowed be your name. Help us, Lord, not to misuse your name.

Review questions

1. Why can we call the God of the universe 'Father'?

_____

_____

_____

2. Draw a line connecting each Old Testament Hebrew name for God with its correct English translation:

Hebrew	Translation
Jehovah-tsidkenu	Jehovah My Shepherd
Jehovah-shalom	Jehovah is There
Jehovah-shammah	Jehovah Who Sanctifies
Jehovah-m'kaddesh	Jehovah is Peace
Jehovah-jireh	God's Provision Shall be Seen
Jehovah-rohi	Jehovah My Banner
Jehovah-nissi	Jehovah Heals
Jehovah-rophe	Jehovah My Righteousness

3. Match the letter of each word on the left with the benefit in the New Covenant with which it corresponds:

Word		Benefit
a. Spirit	_____	The promise of forgiveness of sin and deliverance from sin's dominion
b. Soundness	_____	The fulness of the Holy Spirit
c. Sin	_____	The promise of health and healing
d. Success	_____	The promise of freedom from the curse of the law
e. Security	_____	Freedom from the fear of death and hell

4. Cursing and using God's name as a swear word is one way in which people misuse his name. Explain another way we can misuse his name. _____

_____

_____

_____

_____

Prayer Outline

1. Our Father in heaven

   a. Form a mental picture of the blood shed by Jesus on the cross

   b. Thank God that you can call him 'Father' by virtue of that blood

2. Hallowed be your name

   a. Benefit 1: Sin — forgiveness of sin and deliverance from sin's dominion
      - ☐ Hallow his name
      - *Jehovah-tsidkenu:* Jehovah Our Righteousness
      - *Jehovah-m'kaddesh:* Jehovah Who Sanctifies
      - ☐ Make your faith declarations

   b. Benefit 2: Spirit — fulness of the Holy Spirit
      - ☐ Hallow his name
      - *Jehovah-shalom:* Jehovah is Peace
      - *Jehovah-shammah:* Jehovah is There
      - ☐ Make your faith declarations

   c. Benefit 3: Soundness — health and healing
      - ☐ Hallow his name
      - *Jehovah-rophe:* Jehovah Heals
      - ☐ Make your faith declarations

   d. Benefit 4: Success — freedom from the curse
      - ☐ Hallow his name
      - *Jehovah-jireh:* God's Provision Shall be Seen
      - ☐ Make your faith declarations

   e. Benefit 5: Security — freedom from the fear of death and hell
      - ☐ Hallow his name
      - *Jehovah-rohi:* Jehovah My Shepherd
      - *Jehovah-nissi:* Jehovah My Banner
      - ☐ Make your faith declarations

3. Am I misusing the Lord's name?
   a. Ask the Holy Spirit to reveal areas in which you may be misusing the Lord's name
   b. Submit yourself to the lordship of Christ

4. Pray in the Spirit, worshipping and making melody in your heart to the Lord

Part Three

Priorities

*'Your kingdom come,
your will be done'*

10

God's kingdom in you and your family

The *Mekilta,* an ancient manuscript that includes a commentary on most of the book of Exodus, includes this parable:

A man came to a province and asked the people if he could reign over them.

They said, 'What good have you done for us? Why should we accept your reign?'

In response, the man built them a wall. He brought them water. He fought battles for them. Then he asked the question again, 'May I reign over you?'

They responded, 'Yes, yes!'

The parable continues: Thus it was with the Omnipresent. He redeemed Israel from Egypt. He parted the sea for them. He brought them manna.

He provided them with a well. He sent them the quail. He fought the battle of Amalek for them. He said to them, 'May I reign over you?'

They replied, 'Yes, yes!'[1]

The parable stops there, but its application does not. God our Father comes to us and asks, 'May I reign over you?'

Often our audacious reply is, 'Who are you and what good have you done for us that we should accept your reign?'

God need not reply, yet out of love he does: 'I am your Father, the Creator God, who so loved the world that I gave my one and only Son, that whoever believes in him shall not perish but have eternal life. His shed blood brought you righteousness and sanctification,

[1] Brad Young, *The Jewish Background to the Lord's Prayer,* Centre for Judaic-Christian Studies, Austin, Texas, 1984

peace and brought you righteousness and sanctification, peace and access into my presence. With the stripes on his back you were healed and made whole.

'He has redeemed you from the curse of falling short. He sees your needs ahead of time and makes provision for them. He is your banner who goes into battle before you and breaks open the way. You do not have to fear death or hell because he is the Good Shepherd who laid down his life for his sheep, abolished death and brought life and immortality to light.'

Then once more God asks, 'May I reign over you?'

God reigns over us when we obey him, accept his rule and authority in our lives and become active in Jesus' kingdom movement to defeat evil, redeem sinners and bring to humankind the blessings of God's reign. This, essentially, is what we are earnestly desiring when we declare, 'Your kingdom come, your will be done.' We are submitting to God and calling upon him to perform his will on earth.

Consider the verbs in these two statements: 'Your kingdom come, your will be done on earth as it is in heaven.' In the Greek, the verbs are placed at the beginning of these two statements for emphasis. I cannot translate the meaning in any better way than to say that it is like a man firmly, decisively putting his foot down. 'Come, kingdom of God! Be done, will of God!'

Let me illustrate. In a business transaction or in a relationship, have you ever said, 'I'm drawing the line right here. This is the way it's going to be. I'm putting my foot down!'? That is the idea in these two statements. Therefore, it is neither arrogant nor presumptuous to declare boldly, 'Come, kingdom of God! Be done, will of God!'

God has a will for each day of your life; therefore, put your foot down in prayer. Instead of constantly mouthing weak little prayers such as, 'Oh, Jesus, help me,' begin boldly declaring God's promises. Stand in the victory that Christ has won for you. Refuse to let Satan's puny attempts to intimidate you hinder God's mighty purposes. Declare that God's will shall be done, that his kingdom shall come.

And what is the kingdom of God? Paul tells us, 'The kingdom of God is not a matter of eating and drinking, but of righteousness, peace and joy in the Holy Spirit' (Romans 14:17).

We want God's priorities to become established in our lives, but so often 'the tail wags the dog'. Someone has called it 'the tyranny of the urgent', meaning that we allow many things that cause us anxiety and trouble to crowd out the important things, things that should be given top priority.

For example, have you ever buttoned up your jacket and missed the top button? You glanced down, saw everything was out of line and realised you would have to unbutton it and start all over again. Life is like that. If you don't have God as your top priority, nothing else will line up as it should. Your health, emotions, goals and relationships get off centre.

How well I know! In the early years of my marriage and ministry, my time priorities were all out of line. I was a student at a Bible college thirty-five miles away from home, minister of youth and evangelism at Beverly Hills Baptist Church, a husband and the father of three little kids.

When it came to time management, my priorities went something like this: the church came first, my studies came second, my family came third, and prayer and communion with God came last. I knew that Jesus commanded, 'Seek first his kingdom and his righteousness, and all these things will be given to you as well' (Matthew 6:33), but I did just the opposite. I was busy seeking 'all these things' instead of seeking first the kingdom.

But when I put Jesus first, he began to put all the

other things into their proper places, and the confusion and disorder were replaced by the soothing peace of God.

As the years passed by and my schedule became busier and more complicated, it became necessary for me to be away from my family much of the time, but Melva and I knew what to do. We made our schedules a matter of prayer, and God showed us unique solutions for our particular way of life.

What works for me will work for you. As you give priority to prayer and seek God's wisdom, the Lord will begin to correct and realign your schedule, revealing the solutions to your time management problems.

Ordering your *time* priorities is important, but next you must establish *prayer* priorities. As you pray, you must declare that God's kingdom come and his will be done in these four major areas: 1. yourself; 2. your family; 3. your church; 4. your nation. How do you pray over these four important areas?

Just as the set of its rudder determines a ship's course, so the tongue sets the course of one's life, for the tongue is the rudder of life (see James 3:3-5). Although aimless confessions will not accomplish much, when the tongue agrees with the Spirit of God and declares with sincerity and faith, 'Your kingdom come, your will be done,' the correct course of life is set. So every day as you pray, declare that God's kingdom shall come and that his will shall be done in these four major areas.

Yourself

Begin with yourself. James 5:16 says, 'The prayer of a righteous man is powerful and effective.' Unless you are right before God, your prayer will not be effective. Each day pray that God's kingdom — his righteousness, joy and peace — be established in you and that his will for you that day be set in your spirit.

You need divine wisdom and revelation if you are properly to administrate your home, business, resources and so forth. When you pray, 'Your kingdom come, your will be done,' invite Jesus to assume his rightful place on the throne of your heart and to rule your spirit, soul and body. Then pray over the particular concerns in which you will be involved throughout the day.

Ask the Holy Spirit to empower you with ability, efficiency and might. In the words of Jude, 'Build yourselves up . . . make progress, rise like an edifice higher and higher' by 'praying in the Holy Spirit' (Jude 20 Amp). Stay before the Lord until the course of your day is set and the Spirit of God is functioning in you. This is vitally important, for if Jesus is not Lord in *you*, he will not be Lord in your second priority — your family.

Your family

If you are married, pray for your partner. Pray that righteousness, peace and joy will rule your partner's life. Making the declaration of faith 'Your kingdom come, your will be done,' pray over the needs of your partner until the Spirit releases you to move on in prayer. This is vitally important because if you lose your own house, your work for the house of God will be greatly hindered.

A young evangelist on the verge of losing his wife seemed more concerned about his reputation and the evangelistic meetings he had scheduled than in wooing his wife and seeing their marriage restored. As he knelt to pray about the great ministry he wanted to do for God, the Lord put a piercing question to his young servant: 'What makes you think I want to entrust *my* Bride to you when you won't even take care of your own?'

Our families must come first. Some of the most remorseful people I know are individuals who tried to win the world for God but lost their own families in the process.

How should you pray for your family? If you have children, declare, 'Your kingdom come, your will be done,' in each of their lives. Make specific petitions. Listen to what the Spirit of God speaks to you regarding your children.

The Lord began speaking to me about our son, John Aaron, while he was still in his mother's womb, and everything the Spirit of God said to me is coming to pass in his life.

When he was eleven, John Aaron said, 'Dad, do you remember Mike, the boy at school whom nobody likes because he's dyslexic? He can't read, and the kids say he's stupid. Well, today I led him to Jesus.'

Do you know why that happened? Because every day of John Aaron's life I have declared, 'Your kingdom come in him, Lord. Will of God, be done in him!' Every day I pray over my son and my two daughters, Joanna and Joy Elizabeth, and make that declaration over them.

I also pray over the individuals each of them may eventually marry and pray that they will not get out of the perfect will of God for their lives. Why? Because I've seen that it pays to pray like that.

Here's the best illustration I know of praying for your children and those whom they will marry:

My wife, Melva Jo, has her master's degree in music; she is an operatic soprano, an incredible vocalist who has sung all over the world. We met when we were in college. She was Miss Dallas Baptist College, and I was a 'mole in a hole'. (I was busy reading the red and praying for the power, remember?)

Here she was, the socialite of the campus, singing for the president of the Southern Baptist Convention, and here I was, just a little old guy who couldn't match my socks. We were both in the college choir, so I had noticed her, of course. But I was dating a girl back in my hometown, and Melva was engaged to a guy in Mississippi.

Our choir travelled all over the world that year, and Melva and I became friends. One evening she and I were in my car heading for a concert when she casually announced, 'Well, I'm gonna get married.'

I grinned and said, 'You ought to marry that poor guy, Melva. You've been engaged to him for three years.'

Melva was silent for a minute, then answered quietly, 'Yes, but I'm not going to marry *him*.'

Something in the way she said that made something inside of me go 'Doi-yoi-yoi-yoing!' I didn't say a word and neither did she, but it must have hit her, too, because she didn't want me to drive her back to the college that night. Actually, she did something really mature: here she was a senior in college, and she hid in the bathroom so I couldn't find her.

And the next day? Well, then she wouldn't go to class because she didn't want to face me. But I knew where she worked, so I did something really mature, too. I went there and hid behind a tree. When she finished work, I jumped out in front of her and commanded, 'Melva Jo Bryant, don't you go anywhere.'

She smiled, ducked her head and said softly, 'I'm not going anywhere.'

We went to a quiet hillside to talk. The sun was setting, and it was so romantic. Like Simon Peter not knowing what to say on the Mount of Transfiguration, I blurted out, 'Do you realise we could get married?' (That was one of the first serious things I had ever said to her.)

Returning my gaze, she said thoughtfully, 'Yes, I guess so. Larry, if this is really the Lord, my fiance will call and break up with me.'

You guessed it. Three days later that dude called her. 'Melva,' he confessed, 'I've been wanting to call for several weeks now, but I didn't want to break your heart. You see, I'm going out with a girl here in Mississippi, and I want to break my engagement to you. I don't think we should get married.'

He must have been shocked by the tone in Melva's reply. 'Good!' she said, breathing a prayer of thanks. 'Good!'

Melva came to me and told me what had happened, adding emphatically: 'This is the Lord's will.'

I thought, 'I'm too young to die!'

Then Melva announced, 'We've got to talk to my dad.'

'Your dad?' I mumbled, trying not to choke.

So we drove off to the hills of Arkansas where Melva had grown up. Late that night we arrived at her parents' home, where they greeted us at the door. Melva introduced me and announced proudly, 'Dad, this is the man I'm going to marry.'

Mr Bryant stared at me and sputtered, 'That? That? That's what I've prayed for — for almost forty years?' (That's not the whole truth, but it went something like that.)

Then he sat me down at their breakfast table and told me a story I'll never forget.

'Son,' he began kindly, 'Melva's mother was told that it was medically impossible for her ever to bear a child. But we cried out to God as Hannah did for Samuel. For twenty years we prayed, "God, give us a child. Your will be done over our child." After twenty years of marriage, we made a vow to God. We promised, "God, if the child you give us is a boy, we will dedicate him to the ministry. If it's a girl, we'll dedicate her to be a pastor's wife."'

Mr Bryant paused, and I thought, 'I never even had a chance!'

Then Melva's dad continued the story. 'When my wife was forty years old, she conceived for the first time. For seven of the nine months of pregnancy she lay flat on her back in bed. But when she gave birth to a healthy girl, we held our baby up before the Lord and vowed, "Jesus, every day of her life we will declare that the will of God be done in our child." '

Don't you see? Melva's decision, 'I'm not going to marry him,' was the forty-year composite of her parents' putting their foot down in prayer and declaring, 'Your will be done in the life of our daughter, Lord.'

That's why I urge you to intercede for your children and to pray that they will not get out of the perfect will of God for their lives. While your children are young, ask God to reveal his plans for their futures in order that you can train them up in the way they should go. Treasure in your heart those things the Lord speaks to you about each child, and claim God's wisdom daily in guiding and training your children.

Petition the Lord to lay other family members upon your heart. Allow the circle of your concern and compassion to be enlarged.

At times you are sure to get 'hung up' in prayer, unable to leave one person. When that happens, be sensitive to the Holy Spirit because he knows that the person needs prayer that day. Make sure you don't rush through some little prayer formula, but pray until the Holy Spirit gives you release.

If your prayer time is gone and you haven't prayed through all the topics in the Lord's Prayer, stop and then pick up the prayer outline where you left off at the first opportunity later in the day — driving your car, working around the house, before going to sleep. Let your life become a life of prayer. Learn to 'pray the price' for what you need.

And every day as God asks, 'May I reign in you?' joyfully declare: 'Yes, yes! Your kingdom come, Lord. Your will be done. I call upon you to perform your perfect will in me, in my partner and children and in my loved ones. I place your will before my own desires.'

There are other important priorities yet to be established and maintained. Let's consider these next as we, with intense inward yearning, continue to pray this powerful plea: 'Your kingdom come, your will be done!'

11

God's kingdom in your church and nation

In 1974 I interviewed Richard Wurmbrand, a Jewish Christian who had spent three years in a Romanian dungeon where he was tortured for his faith.

'Mr Wurmbrand,' I asked, 'do you think American Christians are going to experience what you experienced?'

His reply startled me. 'No,' he answered thoughtfully, 'I don't think it's *going* to come. I think it's already here. In America, I experience ten times more demonic spiritual oppression fighting to make me draw back than I ever experienced in a dungeon.'

It is an indisputable fact. As believers, you and I are part of God's army, and it is at war. It's time we realised that God's army was formed to fight, not to show off our shiny brass buttons and polished boots. God has called us to be warriors — to be an anointed, delivering army with healing in our hands. We can lose by default, but we *cannot* lose if we will fight.

Paul, one of God's generals, commanded us to 'fight the good fight of the faith' (1 Timothy 6:12). Notice that Paul didn't say, 'Fight if you feel like it. Fight if you have that sort of personality.' Every believer must fight the good fight of faith. Satan has declared war on believers, and he doesn't fight fair.

The devil doesn't bat a bloodshot eye at attacking the harmless, the innocent or the inexperienced in battle. You and your family are just as much Satan's prey as your church and your nation are. Therefore, it is of critical importance that you learn how to pray daily over four vital areas and declare, 'Come, kingdom of God! Be done, will of God!'

We have talked about how you can establish and maintain godly priorities in yourself and your family. Now turn your attention to two other critical areas, your church and your nation, and let's discover how to defeat the devil there.

Your church

Your third prayer priority is your church. Pray for the pastor, the leadership of the church, the faithfulness of the people and the harvest.

Pastor

As you pray for your pastor, ask God to anoint him, speak to him and direct him. Petition the Lord to give your pastor a shepherd's heart, to impart wisdom to him as he spends time in the Word and in prayer, and to make him a pure channel through which the gifts and power of the Holy Spirit can flow.

Leadership

Say the leaders' names in prayer. As you pray for them one by one, the Holy Spirit will often show you specific needs. Pray for the people in the church who are ministering in ways which touch your own life directly. Pray that the Lord will make the various groups and organisations in the church healthy. Ask the Lord to show them how to breathe in through fellowship and breathe out in evangelism.

Faithfulness

Pray that the people of the church will be faithful to their families, to the vision God has given your church, and to Jesus. Entreat the Holy Spirit to plant them in the house of the Lord so that they will bring forth fruit as soulwinners and intercessors. Pray that they will be faithful in bringing their tithes and offerings into the storehouse and that they will serve God as he deserves to be served.

Harvest

God gave me a passage from Isaiah to claim when praying in the harvest for the church: 'Do not be afraid, for I am with you; I will bring your children from the east and gather you from the west. I will say to the north, "Give them up!" and to the south, "Do not hold them back." Bring my sons from afar and my daughters from the ends of the earth — everyone who is called by my name, whom I created for my glory, whom I formed and made' (Isaiah 43:5-7).

Therefore, as I pray over my church, I speak to the powers and principalities of the air who work in the children of disobedience (see Ephesians 2:2). These powers and principalities hold the reins over certain areas, so I speak to the area north of my church as if it were a person and say, 'North, you have people whom God wills to become a part of my church. I command you in the name of Jesus to release every person who is supposed to become a part of this body.'

Then I speak to the south, east and west, and in the Spirit I look them right in the face. I command them to release *every* one — not every other one — that God has ordained to be saved, planted, strengthened and established in my church.

I tarry there in prayer until I have a release in my spirit that the evil powers are listening and relinquishing what belongs to me. Through the Spirit, I face those geographical areas and challenge them until they drop the reins of control. Then in Jesus' name, I ask God to dispatch angels to minister to the heirs of salvation (see Hebrews 1:13-14).

Now that may sound 'far out' to some people. But let's not fall into the habit of labelling every slightly out-of-the-ordinary approach we run up against as the sure sign of a counterfeit; it may be the real thing. Remember how unorthodox Jesus' methods seemed to the Pharisees who perceived themselves to be spiritual experts.

As Donald Gee, a wise British pastor and Bible teacher for many years, once said, 'Those who pretend to pass judgment in spiritual matters must be prepared to show their credentials of personal spiritual experience.'[1] Unfortunately, many people condemning manifestations and experiences birthed by the Holy Spirit have had little personal experience with either.

How many of you know that Jesus Christ is the same yesterday, today and for ever? And how many of you also know that the Pharisees are the same yesterday, today and for ever! Let's not be spiritually ignorant and naive. Let's desire to be balanced, not embalmed. Now get a good grip on your theological hat, because I've got something else to say!

One day when I was praying intently in the Spirit and commanding the north to give up everyone who belonged to my church, I saw a vision of a huge, black, moss-covered, Darth-Vader-looking creature. He stood at least nine feet tall, and he held a chain. The demonic creature sneered at me in contempt, beckoning to me, mocking me, as if to say, 'Are you really serious? Are you willing to fight me over this?'

Something stood straight up in my spirit, and I knew how David must have felt as he faced Goliath. I heard myself backing him down, declaring that he *would* release every soul the Holy Spirit was drawing to become a part of God's church. He stared at me as I resisted him in the name of Jesus, then he slowly dropped the chain and backed off.

Close to that time, something else happened. One morning I was speaking to the north, south, east and west, commanding them to give up. Just then, I saw a vision of a huge, marching army. I'm talking about tens of thousands! They were wearing battle fatigues and marching in perfect time.

[1] *Concerning Spiritual Gifts*, by Donald Gee, Gospel Publishing House, Springfield, Missouri, 1972

Amazed, I asked, 'Lord, what's that?'

The Lord replied, 'Son, that's your church.'

At that time, our church had only about three hundred people, so I gasped incredulously, 'My church?'

Later, the Lord spoke again and explained, 'Larry, when you pray that the east will give up, you're thinking about the Texas towns of Greenville and Sulphur Springs, less than fifty miles away, but when I say east, I'm thinking about Germany. I'm talking about Jerusalem. I'm the God of the whole earth.'

I laughed and really got a kick out of that. I even shared it with the intercessors in our early morning prayer meeting, and we all laughed about God thinking of Germany when we declared, 'East, give up! Don't keep back!'

The next Sunday as I gave the invitation at the close of the service, I said, 'All week I've prayed over you people, and I know you are here from the north, south, east and west, because we've prayed you in. The Bible says the Lord added to the church daily such as should be saved. How many of you feel today that the Lord is adding you to this church? Will you please raise your hand and then come down to the front here so I can pray over you?'

Among those who walked down the aisle was a handsome six-foot-four man with his beautiful blonde wife and two cute little boys. The Spirit of God whispered to me, 'Ask him where they're from.'

Obediently, I singled out the man and enquired, 'Sir, would you tell me where you're from?'

He almost clicked his heels together and saluted! He said, 'Two years ago while I was serving in Germany as a major in the US Army, I heard one of your tapes about praying over the north, south, east and west. The Lord told me to resign my commission in the army, move to Rockwall, Texas, and join the army of God here.'

Folks, this is real stuff! We must learn to pray and obey, as Paul Yonggi Cho said years ago, and God will take care of the details. It wasn't a beautiful building or some perfectly orchestrated programme that added over four thousand new members to Church on the Rock in 1985. In one three-month period in 1986 we saw over five hundred people born again. That spiritual momentum continues to build. That's not Larry Lea; that's God.

God has taught us first to pray and command the north, south, east and west to give up. Then we ask the Holy Spirit to draw souls to Jesus, and we release angels to minister to the heirs of salvation. We pray, 'Don't let the people have accidents while they're on their way to church. Don't let things provoke families to arguments and prevent their coming to God's house. Minister grace to the people as they're driving here.' And last, we declare the faith level given to us by God.

What do I mean by that? When I speak of faith levels, I'm not referring to 'hype', 'positive mental attitude' or man-made and man-motivated objectives. I'm talking about Spirit-imparted goals. You see, the Spirit of God puts into my spirit a specific number of souls I'm to ask God for. I share it with my staff, and we begin to ask for that specific number of additions. Each morning as we pray, we set ourselves in agreement with God for that particular number of souls to be added to the church.

Through the years, we have noted a marked correlation between the number of faithful intercessors in our early morning prayer meetings, the amount of tithes and offerings given and the number of people added to the church.

For instance, in 1984 we had about twenty faithful intercessors at morning prayer. (We had more people praying, but I'm talking about faithful prayer warriors.) Our offerings were around twenty thousand dollars weekly, and about twenty people joined the church each week.

The number of intercessors grew, and about midway through 1984 God said, 'I want you to believe me for sixty new members and sixty thousand dollars a week.' We began having about sixty faithful intercessors, the offerings grew to sixty thousand dollars weekly, and we averaged sixty new additions to our church each week.

The number of faithful intercessors climbed, and in 1985 our faith level was for a hundred additions to the church and one hundred and ten thousand dollars each week. God brought it to pass, and this spiritual correlation continues.

Today we have many more prayer warriors. Entire families come to the church for morning prayer, and many members of our church who live too far away to drive to Rockwall each morning for prayer have begun morning prayer meetings in their homes.

I'm not promising that the same thing will happen in your church, but I'll tell you this: if I were you, I would ask the Holy Spirit to purify my motives. Then I would help begin an early morning prayer meeting in my church if it didn't already have one, and release God to do what he wants to do in your midst.

Make prayer for your church a priority. Pray for the pastor and leadership. Pray for the faithfulness of the people and for the harvest, and declare, 'Come, kingdom of God. Be done, will of God!'

Your nation

Your fourth prayer priority is your nation. Pray that the Prime Minister will have the wisdom of God; that spiritual leaders will walk in wisdom, be people of prayer and be kept by the power of God. Pray specifically, naming your local and national leaders. Intercede for the UK. Pray for revival.

The Lord also commands us to pray for the peace of Jerusalem (Psalm 122:6), so pray for the nation of Israel.

You may wish to ask God to lay another nation of the world upon your heart — communist nations, countries experiencing revolution or famine, and so forth. Allow the Spirit of God to enlarge your borders of concern and compassion.

At this point, you will have prayed through the first two topics in Christ's model prayer: 'Our Father in heaven, hallowed be your name'; and 'Your kingdom come, your will be done on earth as it is in heaven.' There are four remaining demarcations.

Perhaps you now realise how simple it is to pray one hour. You are learning how to pray for multitudes of things that once caused you fear, worry and frustration. And now instead of thinking, 'How could I ever pray for an entire hour?' you may be wondering, 'How can I ever get through it in only one hour?'

You see, our problem has been simple. Not knowing what to say or do when we prayed, we wore ourselves out in about ten minutes. But Jesus said, 'This is how you should pray,' and he gave us a prayer outline to follow.

In the context of this prayer are the five major themes that have been restored to vitality in the church in our time. They are praise and worship, kingdom authority, prosperity, relationships and spiritual authority. Each of those themes is there, and each is in perfect balance.

Yes, in the context of this prayer is everything you need in order to live full and free in spiritual victory!

Review questions

1. The _____ is the rudder of life (James 3:3-5).

2. What is the kingdom of God? Romans 14:17 declares, 'The kingdom of God is not a matter of eating and drinking, but of _____ , _____ and _____ in the Holy Spirit.'

3. What are four major areas in which God's kingdom should be established?

   a. _____

   b. _____

   c. _____

   d. _____

4. Unless you are right before God your prayer will not be effective, for the Bible says, 'The prayer of a _____ man is powerful and effective' (James 5:16).

5. Your third priority is your church. What four specific areas should be covered when you pray for your church?

   a. _____

   b. _____

   c. _____

   d. _____

6. As a reminder to yourself, in the space provided below list specific people and topics for which you personally want to pray when you come to the fourth priority, your nation:

   _____

   _____

   _____

   _____

7. Can you think of time you spend doing unimportant, unnecessary things during the course of your day that could be devoted to prayer? If so, list those times here and ask the Holy Spirit to help you and remind you to redeem that time.

   _____

   _____

   _____

Prayer outline

1. Make a declaration of faith: 'Your kingdom come, your will be done — not simply willed — but done'

2. Four major areas to establish his kingdom

   a. Yourself

   ☐ Be sure you are right before God

☐ Ask Jesus to be seated on the throne of your life and to rule in every area
☐ Abide before the Lord until the course of your day is set and the Spirit of God is functioning in you

b. Your family
☐ Partner
☐ Children
☐ Other family members

c. Your church
☐ Your pastor
☐ Leadership of the church
☐ Faithfulness of the people
☐ The harvest

d. Nation
☐ Local and national political leaders
☐ Spiritual leaders
☐ Revival

3. Ask the Spirit of God:

a. To implement your priorities
b. To help you live them out

Part Four

Provision
*'Give us today our
daily bread'*

12

Being in God's will

A third-year Bible college student rarely dines at the exclusive Petroleum Club in Fort Worth, Texas, but I was in those elegant surroundings at the invitation of the wealthy gentleman seated across the table.

After grace, I reached for my fork, then paused in surprise. He was crying. This distinguished, respected, sixty-year-old millionaire bowed his head, and hot tears dripped off his chin, staining his expensive silk tie.

'Sir,' I said softly, 'what's wrong? Can I help?'

Several seconds elapsed as he struggled to regain his composure. Taking a deep breath, he confided, 'I was nineteen years old when God called me to preach, but I said no. I wanted my own way, wanted to make a lot of money. So I refused to take my hands off my life.'

His voice broke, and more tears trickled down his face. 'But I don't have any peace,' he sobbed brokenly. 'I missed God's purpose for my life.'

I can't help imagining that the scene I witnessed that day was a repeat performance of a similar role that might have been played by another wealthy aristocrat in his latter days — the man whom we have come to know as the 'rich young ruler'.

You remember the story. Jesus was on his way to Jerusalem when a well-dressed young man came running up and fell at Jesus' feet. 'Good teacher,' he asked earnestly, 'what must I do to inherit eternal life?'

Mark records the momentous decision that took place in the next few moments: 'Jesus looked at him and loved him. "One thing you lack," he said. "Go, sell everything you have and give to the poor, and you will have treasure in heaven. Then come, follow me.'' At this the man's face fell. He went away sad, because he had great wealth' (Mark 10:17-22).

The rich young ruler was a good man, a religious man, but there was something amiss. Jesus knew what it was, and he put his finger on it: the love of money. When he instructed the young man to sell out and follow him, Jesus wasn't trying to rip the guy off. He was trying to prevent him from trusting in his riches. Jesus was offering the man the soundest investment counselling he would ever receive, but he refused it and walked away.

God's principles are diametrically opposed to those of the world. God says, 'Give, and it will be given to you.' The world cautions, 'Get all you can, and can all you get!' But man's ways are not God's ways.

Have you ever noticed the beautiful balance in the Lord's Prayer? The first concern is *his name;* the second is *his kingdom and his will.* Then he tells us to pray, *'Give us* today our daily bread.' If we seek first God's kingdom and his righteousness, all the other things will be added to us. We must understand that Jesus wasn't trying to transform the rich young ruler into the poor old beggar. He was trying to break the power of the greed and poverty that bound this young man's soul.

The rich young ruler's purpose was to count his money at night. He built his life around his money. A lot of people are like that. They have their security cushions, but they can't sleep at night or enjoy their slap-up meals. God wants to free his children from that suffocating mindset.

It is no surprise that God's four basic requirements for successfully praying in what we need are not what the natural man would guess readily. What are those requirements? First, you must *be in the will of God.* Second, you must *believe it is God's will to prosper you.*

Third, you must *be specific* when you pray daily for what you need. And fourth, you must be *tenacious*.

Be in the will of God

Being in the will of God implies four things: 1. fellowship with Jesus through prayer and reading the Word of God; 2. fellowship with God's church; 3. diligent, balanced work habits; 4. obedience in giving.

Fellowship with Jesus

To be in the will of God, daily fellowship with Jesus in the Word and in prayer is essential.

If, like the rich young ruler, you have religion but not a relationship with God, you will not experience God's peace, purpose or power. But as you fellowship with Jesus, the Holy Spirit empowers you with divine ability, efficiency and might to do the will of God (see Acts 1:8 Amp).

Fellowship with one another

The story is told of a woman who walked up to Dwight L. Moody at the conclusion of a service and said, 'Mr Moody, I want to sing in your choir.'

Moody enquired, 'Who is your pastor? Where is your local church?'

The woman stuck her nose in the air and replied smugly, 'I don't have a local church or a pastor. I'm a member of the great universal church.'

Moody thought about it for a second and said, 'You go and find the pastor of the great universal church and sing in his choir.'

Now Moody wasn't being rude; he was being realistic, for the Word of God commands: 'Obey your leaders and submit to their authority. They keep watch over you as men who must give an account. Obey them so that their work will be a joy, not a burden, for that would be of no advantage to you' (Hebrews 13:17).

It is God's will that we be rightly related to our

brothers and sisters in a local church. We should also be committed and submitted to our pastor. We are commanded not to forsake the assembling of ourselves together; instead, we are to exhort one another (see Hebrews 10:25 RAV). *Exhort* means 'to admonish, to urge one to pursue some future course of conduct'. Isn't it wonderful to have fellowship with believers who can impel us morally, encourage and urge us forward and stimulate us to good works?

Balanced, diligent work habits
The next prerequisite to being in the will of God is to have diligent, balanced work habits.

Paul gave instructions regarding work (see 1 Thessalonians 4:11-12). We are to earn our living with our own hands and command the respect of the outside world as we are self-supporting and have need of nothing. Paul warned us not to be neglectful of duty and pass our lives in idleness, being busy with other people's affairs instead of our own, thus doing no work (see 2 Thessalonians 3:11-12). As a matter of fact, Paul commanded: 'If a man will not work, he shall not eat' (2 Thessalonians 3:10).

As pastor of a church, I've noticed that we human beings seem to be divided into two groups: givers and takers. I know for a fact that there are seasons when God may lead a believer to live by faith, and then he will even send ravens to feed that believer if necessary. However, far too often, the brother or sister who asserts, 'God told me to live by faith,' is actually saying, 'I want to live on *your* faith.'

That's one side of the coin. But the other side of the coin is also a problem. Too many believers are working two jobs in order to keep up with the Joneses and dress their kids in designer jeans. We need to be real! We sing, 'When we've been there ten thousand years, bright shining as the sun', without a thought that the material things for which we neglect the kingdom of God and work so hard will be vapour in ten thousand years.

Some believers are workaholics who allow the cares of this life and the deceitfulness of riches to choke out the Word of God and render their lives fruitless (see Matthew 13:22). Pride, fear, worry and insecurity drive us to overwork, but when we realise that God our Father is our source — not ourselves or pay-cheques or savings accounts — we can be content to do the possible and let him do the impossible.

Obedience in giving
The fourth prerequisite to being in the will of God is obedience in giving.

In Malachi 3:10, God promises that if we bring our tithes into the storehouse, he will open the windows of heaven and pour out so many blessings we cannot contain them. Acknowledging God as our source and giving unselfishly back to him helps destroy the root of all evil, the love of money (see 1 Timothy 6:10). If we take care of the *root* of evil, we will not have the *fruit* of evil in our lives.

God promises that if we bring our tithes into the storehouse, he will pour out blessings upon us. On the other hand, in Malachi 3:8-9, he promises curses if we rob him of tithes and offerings. God will not bless something he has cursed. Obedience in giving is essential if we are to receive God's best.

We also need to realise that there is a proper order to giving and receiving. First, we give that there may be meat in *God's* house; then he blesses *our* house. First we give; then it is given to us (see Luke 6:38). As we seek first the kingdom of God and his righteousness, all these things will be given to us as well (Matthew 6:33).

When we give to God first, rather than hoarding our limited resources, we acknowledge that he is our source. Remember: we cannot claim God's blessings if we are violating this basic principle of prosperity.

We must also obey God when he asks us to give the unusual or unexpected. I learned that one the hard way. Perhaps you can learn from my mistakes.

I was a twenty-four-year-old married man when I went to India to minister. While there I prayed for a seventeen-year-old girl who had been blind for ten years. God instantly healed her, and the entire village turned to God because of that miracle.

I had the privilege of ministering in villages where the people had never heard the gospel preached. One day as I walked along a dusty road, the Holy Spirit asked, 'What would you say if I told you, just as Jesus told the rich young ruler, to sell everything you own? Would you do it and give the money to missions?'

I replied glibly, 'Lord, I'd do anything you tell me to do.' (Let me urge you never to tell God you will do something unless you mean it.)

I just assumed it would be one of those 'Abraham and Isaac' deals where God tested me to see if I was willing and then just dropped the matter. Instead, God commanded, 'Go home and do it!'

At that time, Melva, baby John Aaron and I lived in a tiny second-storey flat. Right beneath us lived seven illegal aliens. I mean, this was no high-class joint. We worked for a church, and all we had was a bed, a sofa, two hundred dollars in savings and a car that wasn't worth repairing.

But when God asked me to sell what we had and give the money to missions, I discovered that people who don't have anything can be just as hung up on their 'stuff' as people who have everything.

When I told Melva what the Lord had told me in India, she didn't feel a confirmation at all. As a matter of fact, she said, 'I don't believe that's God, Larry. Let's pray some more about it.'

So instead of obeying God, we prayed a little about it, and I enrolled in Bible college. But I became physically sick, emotionally sick, and I was so depressed for six months that I hardly made it.

One Sunday morning I was too ill to go to church, so I sat at home watching evangelist James Robison on television. Suddenly, James whirled around, pointed at the camera and announced emphatically: 'There's a man listening to me who wants to be a prophet of God. God has already told you what to do, and you haven't obeyed him. Mister, you will remain sick and stay at home until you do what God told you to do.'

His long, skinny finger seemed to point through the screen right at me! So do you know what I did the next day? I got myself a Loadlugger trailer and loaded up everything we had in the house.

My father-in-law met me at the front door. (You remember him and the tremendous first impression I had made on him?) Making every effort to stay calm and uninvolved, he stuffed his hands in his pockets and asked, 'What are you doing, son?'

I replied, 'I'm loading up all our furniture, and I'm going to sell it and send the money to India.'

His eyes widened and he choked out, 'What did you say?'

But I had made up my mind. I was tired of not doing what Jesus had told me to do. Melva cried a little as she helped me load it all up, bless her heart, but we obeyed.

It wasn't easy. Melva and John Aaron and I slept on the floor for a while. Before you shake your head and mutter, 'What a fanatic,' let me tell you the rest of the story.

Two years later, while we were still working on that same church staff, we made our final payment on a home costing forty-nine thousand dollars. It happened supernaturally. Why? Because God said, 'Give, and it will be given to you. A good measure, pressed down, shaken together and running over, will be poured into your lap. For with the measure you use, it will be measured to you' (Luke 6:38). That's the perfect way to describe God's abundant provision for me and my family through the years.

And if you're wondering about my relationship with my father-in-law, let me assure you that we share a mutual love and respect for each other. He and Melva's mum moved to Rockwall so that they could be near us and their grandchildren, and the two of them have won a special place in the hearts of our congregation at Church on the Rock.

It's really very simple. The requirements for being in the will of God can be reduced to one element: the lordship of Jesus Christ in your life. If he is Lord, you will have fellowship with him in a personal prayer life and in the Word. You will have fellowship with his church. You will be diligent and balanced in your work habits, and you will be obedient in giving. If these basic prerequisites to being in the will of God are established in your life, you can depend on God to supply all your needs.

That's the first requirement for praying in God's provision. There are three more. As we discuss them, mentally 'grade' yourself and look for weak areas you may need to strengthen in order to pray more effectively, 'Give us today our daily bread.'

13

Meeting God's requirements

My father made a fortune in oil and gas in Texas, so I grew up surrounded by luxury. But because 'stuff' had never satisfied, I reacted against wealth and concluded that anybody who had money and 'stuff' couldn't be right with God.

But the more I studied the Bible, the more it defied my philosophy. When I opened the Bible, I thought I would find a bunch of impoverished ascetics. Instead, I read about wealthy Abraham (see Genesis 24:35). I read about Abraham's son, Isaac, who sowed and reaped a hundredfold during a time of famine and accumulated great possessions (see Genesis 26:1, 12-14). As I studied the lives of King David and his son, Solomon, I shook my head in amazement at their tremendous wealth.

Then I read about Job and how he lost everything, and I thought, 'Now we're getting on the right track.' But Job 42:10 reveals that God turned the captivity of Job and gave him twice as much as he had before.

I read the words of Moses in Deuteronomy 8:18: 'Remember the Lord your God, for *it is he who gives you the ability to produce wealth*, and so confirms his covenant.' I studied the promises in Malachi 3, referring to the giving of tithes and offerings.

Then I got into the New Testament and saw the promise of Jesus: 'Give, and it will be given to you. A good measure, pressed down, shaken together and running over, will be poured into your lap. For with the measure you use, it will be measured to you' (Luke 6:38).

And I discovered his pledge to those who sacrifice for the sake of the gospel: 'No-one who has left home or brothers or sisters or mother or father or children or fields for me and the gospel will fail to receive a hundred times as much in this present age (homes, brothers, sisters, mothers, children and fields — and with them, persecutions) and in the age to come, eternal life' (Mark 10:29-30).

At about that time, I discovered the second requirement for praying in God's provision. You must believe that it is God's will to prosper you.

Believe it is God's will to prosper you

Where did we ever get the idea that it was Jesus who came to steal, kill and destroy? 'The blessing of the Lord brings wealth, and he adds no trouble to it' (Proverbs 10:22). Paul promised, 'My God will meet all your needs according to his glorious riches in Christ Jesus' (Philippians 4:19).

Some people have taken these truths concerning prosperity and gone off on a selfish 'bless-me' tangent. But that doesn't negate God's promises. Our Father has made this promise to his faithful children who seek his blessings in order that they might be able to stretch out filled hands to the needy:

'God is able to make all grace (every favour and earthly blessing) come to you in abundance, so that you may always and under all circumstances and whatever the need, be self-sufficient — possessing enough to require no aid or support and furnished in abundance for every good work and charitable donation . . . . And [God] who provides seed for the sower and bread for eating will also provide and multiply your [resources for] sowing, and increase the fruits of your righteousness [which manifests itself in active goodness, kindness and charity]. Thus you will be enriched in all things and in every way, so that you can be generous' (2 Corinthians 9:8, 10-11 Amp).

God doesn't bless us so that we can tear down our old barns and build bigger ones. Believers sometimes misunderstand the purpose of God's blessings and drown in their own gravy.

God knows that money is a necessity. Would it shock you to learn that the Bible says more about money than anything else? The Scriptures are replete with instructions on how to make, save, give and manage money. You see, God wants his children to be givers, not takers; to be the head, and not the tail; to be lenders, not borrowers.

If you aren't already obeying God's command to tithe, why not begin right now? Don't be like the rich young ruler who walked away sorrowful. Sell out to Jesus, and watch him rebuke your devourer. Get the doubt out. Believe that it is God's will to prosper you, then claim his promises for your needs. Daily ask for your allotted portion necessary to fulfil God's plan for your life.

What have we discussed so far? First, in order to pray in God's provision, you have to be in the will of God. Second, you must believe that it is God's will to prosper you. These are extremely important requirements for 'praying in' what you need, but they are incomplete without two additional steps. You must be specific when you pray, and you must be tenacious.

Be specific

A third aspect of praying in God's provision is making specific requests. Do you bring specific needs to God each day, or do you just expect the answers to come in? Jesus instructed us to pray, 'Give us today our daily bread.' By this we know we are to pray daily over our specific needs.

Immediately after Jesus gave his disciples the Lord's Prayer in Luke 11, he related a parable illustrating the importance of asking specifically. Pay close attention to his words: 'Suppose one of you has a friend, and he goes to him at midnight and says, "Friend, lend me three loaves of bread, because a friend of mine on a journey has come to me, and I have nothing to set before him"' (Luke 11:5-6).

Did you catch it? Did you notice that the man asked specifically for three loaves of bread? When you pray, 'Give us today our daily bread,' ask specifically!

If you had to have over a hundred and twelve thousand dollars every week to meet your budget, would it make you nervous? That's what I face every Monday morning, but I don't worry about it. Why? Because over a thousand members of our church are daily agreeing with me in prayer, asking specifically for that amount to come in.

First you must pray specific prayers over the needs of the house of God, then pray specifically for the needs of your own house. When you have sown your financial seed into his kingdom and have been faithful to God and to your church, you can confidently ask for your specific needs.

Be tenacious

In Luke 18:1-8, Jesus told the parable of the unjust judge and the widow who repeatedly, persistently begged, 'Grant me justice against my adversary.' Because of the woman's tenacity, the unrighteous judge granted her request. Jesus emphasised this point to his disciples when he asked, 'Will not God bring about justice for his chosen ones, who cry out to him day and night? Will he keep putting them off?' (v7).

It takes tenacity, shameless persistence, to recover what Satan, our adversary, has stolen from us, but today many believers are not aware of that fact. Instead, they search for spiritual shortcuts. Of course, there may be times when we can 'name it and claim it'. But there are also times when we must intercede fervently, for many needs and situations require earnest tenacity before victory comes.

In his valuable book *The Art of Intercession,* Kenneth Hagin, the well-known faith teacher who in his lifetime has spent untold hours in intercession, urges believers to intercede. He explains:

'Here is where some people miss it. They don't hear everything you teach, and they grab some little something and run off with it. There are some things you can pray the prayer of faith on — and you pray one prayer and that's the end of it. You don't have to pray anymore; you just thank God for the answer . . . . But there are other things you cannot pray the prayer of faith on . . . . For God to accomplish what he desires to accomplish . . . the art of intercessory prayer will have to be resurrected.'[1]

Though your answer may be long in coming, be tenacious. When God hears your prayer of faith, the answer is conceived at that moment (see Daniel 10:12-14). If God's response is delayed, continue to carry the petition in your heart. Don't allow yourself to grow weary as you bear the burden. Don't lose heart and give up, for by doing so you will miss the answer God has prepared.

There can be miscarriages in prayer. That thing conceived in the Spirit can be aborted if we cast away our confidence and refuse to wait on the Lord.

The Amplified Bible translates Matthew 7:7: 'Keep on asking and it will be given you; keep on seeking and you will find; keep on knocking [reverently] and the door will be opened to you.' Jesus told his disciples that 'they should always pray and not give up' (Luke 18:1). Remember: God is a rewarder of those who diligently seek him (Hebrews 11:6).

To summarise, in order to appropriate God's provision you must first be in the will of God. Next, you must believe that it is God's will to prosper you. Then you must be specific and tenacious in prayer.

[1] *The Art of Intercession,* by Kenneth Hagin, Kenneth Hagin Ministries, Tulsa, Oklahoma, 1980

This is how Jesus taught us to expect and experience God's provision.

Review questions

1. True or False? In the following blanks write 'T' if you believe the statement to be true, 'F' if you think it is false

a. _____ Being in the will of God is a basic requirement for successfully praying in what you need

b. _____ To be in the will of God, fellowship with Jesus in a consistent personal prayer life and in the Word of God is essential

c. _____ If we are in God's will, we will be rightly related to our brothers and sisters in a local church and be committed and submitted to our pastor

d. _____ Diligent, balanced work habits are important if a person desires to be in the will of God

e. _____ God says we should take care of the needs of our own house first. Then if there is anything left over, we should help take care of the needs of his kingdom

f. _____ To appropriate God's provision, it is important that you believe that it is God's will to prosper you

g. _____ God knows what we need before we ask. Therefore, it is not necessary to ask daily and specifically for what we need

h. _____ We should only ask God for something once. If he wants us to have it, he will give it to us without our having to keep asking

i. _____ There is copious evidence in God's Word that it is his will to bless his people

2. a. In order to appropriate God's provision it is important that we be in the will of God, believe that it is God's will to prosper us, ask God specifically for our daily needs and be tenacious. In which two of these things have you been weakest?

_____

_____

   b. What will you do to correct those weaknesses?

_____

_____

Prayer outline

1. Be in the will of God

a. Ask the Holy Spirit to help you develop a consistent, daily personal prayer life and time in the Word where you fellowship daily with Jesus

b. Pray that the Lord will plant you in your local church and make you a contributing, functioning, healthy part of that body

c. Examine your work habits. Are you slothful? A workaholic? Ask the Lord to give you ability, efficiency, might and balance

d. Examine your giving. Are you obeying the Lord in bringing your tithes and offerings into the storehouse? Or are you greedy, stingy or a poor manager? Do you pay your bills and have a reputation as a fair and honest person who keeps your word? Take time to pray along these lines

2. Believe that it is God's will to prosper you.

a. Memorise Scriptures such as Luke 6:38 and Philippians 4:19 to use as faith declarations as you pray in your provision

b. Meditate upon the Word of God until you truly understand and believe that it is God's will to bless you

3. Be specific

a. Bring specific needs daily before God

b. Decide to pray instead of worry

4. Be tenacious

a. Repossess lost ground that the devil has stolen from you. Discouragement and unbelief have robbed you of answers to prayer. Take up those petitions again and persevere until the answer comes

b. Praise the Lord because he is *Jehovah-jireh:* he sees your need beforehand and makes provision

Part Five

People

*'Forgive us our debts,
as we also have forgiven
our debtors'*

14

Getting along with everyone

'You'll never play basketball for me again!' the coach threatened angrily as he marched me off the court towards the sidelines. But the fury on his face and the determination in his voice let me know this was more than a threat; it was a fact.

Why hadn't the coach asked to hear my side? Hadn't he seen the other kid throw the first punch? And why hadn't he just suspended me for a game or two instead of taking me out of play altogether? Those questions clouded my mind for the rest of the year as I 'rode the bench', but I consoled myself with the thought that I would get to play for another coach in my next academic year.

But it wasn't to be. The coach was promoted right along with me, and I sat on the bench during my first year, and on into my second year. Finally, we got a new coach and I was allowed to play again, but the damage had been done. By that time, tangled roots of bitterness had established themselves deeply in the soil of my heart.

Years later when I was a Bible college student, the Lord convicted me of that bitterness, and I wrote to that coach asking him to forgive me for the grudge I had carried against him.

Why was it so important to ask his forgiveness? As Christians, you and I are in the process of becoming full grown in God. Part of the process of spiritual growth is learning to forgive one another because our relationship to our fellow-men and -women affects our relationship to God. God will not extend mercy to those who refuse to forgive (see Mark 11:25-26 margin).

If husbands and wives learn to say, 'I'm sorry. Please forgive me,' their marriages keep growing. If not, the marriages die. This is true of any relationship; learning to forgive is an essential element of growth.

May I ask you a personal question? Does a dark cloud rise up on the inside of you when you think of certain people? If so, you need to understand that God uses those who sin against us to teach us how to forgive. And we can never forgive others until we know that we ourselves have been forgiven. Because we are forgiven, for Jesus' sake we forgive others.

Can you see why forgiveness is an important key to spiritual liberty, victory and joy?

As you pray, 'Forgive us our debts, as we also have forgiven our debtors,' there are certain things you must do if you want to get along with everyone all the time.

Ask God to forgive you

Often as you thank God for the blood of Jesus, the Holy Spirit puts a finger on some sin you need to confess and forsake. So when you pray, 'Forgive us our debts,' ask God to look into your heart. If unconfessed sin surfaces at this point, confess the sin to God and claim his promise, in 1 John 1:9: 'If we confess our sins, he is faithful and just and will forgive us our sins and purify us from all unrighteousness.'

In that verse the word *confess* means 'to speak the same thing'. In other words, we must agree with what God says about our sin and be willing to turn away from it.

But the debts Jesus refers to when he instructs us to pray, 'Forgive us our debts, as we also have forgiven our debtors,' encompass more than just our sins. The term also refers to personal debts or moral obligations connected to our relationships with others. That brings us to the second thing we must do if we expect to get along with everyone all the time.

Forgive as often as you want to be forgiven

Take a moment to study this question which Peter put to Jesus: 'Lord, how many times shall I forgive my brother when he sins against me? Up to seven times?' How would you have answered?

Listen to Christ's reply: 'I tell you, not seven times, but seventy-seven times' (Matthew 18:21-22). What was Jesus saying? He was teaching: Forgive as many times as you are offended. Why would Jesus make such a statement? Because that is how many times he is ready and willing to forgive us.

Next, Jesus told Peter a parable which reveals tremendously important truths about forgiveness. This familiar story is found in Matthew 18:23-35, and it teaches a great deal about forgiveness.

First, Jesus uses the parable to teach us that God has forgiven our great debt of sin — a debt so huge that it would be absolutely impossible for us ever to repay it. The servant in this parable owed the king ten thousand talents, approximately £7 million. But the king forgave the servant and cancelled his enormous debt.

That's not the end of the story, though. A fellow-servant owed the forgiven servant a debt of a hundred denarii (about £13), and the forgiven servant made a moral decision not to forgive the debt of his fellow-servant; instead, he had him thrown into prison.

What is the truth conveyed here? That our debt against God is greater than any debt a person will ever owe us and that when we refuse to forgive another person, we place that individual in bondage.

When the king heard what had happened, he asked the forgiven servant a question which is one of the most pivotal in the New Testament, for it is God's question to each one of us: 'Shouldn't you have had

mercy on your fellow-servant just as I had on you?'
(v33). This tells us that we are to forgive at the same
level as we are forgiven by God.

Once we realise how much *we* have been forgiven
by God, we can freely forgive others. If you have
trouble forgiving, ask God to give you a revelation of
Calvary and the price his Son paid for your
forgiveness.

Jesus concludes the parable by describing the king's
anger towards the unforgiving servant. The king
delivers the servant to the tormentors. The lesson? If
we don't forgive, God will deliver us to tormentors
until we choose to forgive others.

You might as well get this straight. If you do not
forgive, you will live with tormenting memories and
demonic oppression until you release the person and
forgive. If you don't forgive, Oral Roberts, Billy
Graham, Kenneth Hagin and James Robison could
agree in prayer and dump two five-gallon buckets of
twenty-forty oil on you, but you would remain in
torment. Why? Because deliverance will not come
until you choose to forgive.

Maintain a right attitude towards others
How is it possible to have a right attitude towards
everyone all the time when some people are hovering
around like vultures waiting for you to fail?

The meaning of the Hebrew word translated 'enemy'
in the Old Testament is 'observer' — someone who is
critically watching. There are always people waiting
to point out your faults, hoping you will fail. So how
do you maintain a right attitude?

The key to a right attitude is preparation. Don't put
off deciding how you will react to those who wrong
you until the hot breath of the enemy is steaming up
your glasses. Each morning before you walk out of
your door, make a wilful decision that you will
respond with love and forgiveness towards those who

offend you. Decide that you will not allow un-forgiveness to rob your spirit of victory, joy and peace.

That simple decision can save you a lot of grief. How do I know? Because I have let unforgiveness rip me off, and it was no fun.

After my room-mate Jerry Howell and I were filled with the Holy Spirit at Dallas Baptist College, things didn't run too smoothly. We lived in a dorm with four hundred and thirty Baptist preachers, and most of them didn't like what we had. It wasn't that Jerry and I were running around trying to promote our experience as the ultimate doctrine in the theological world; it was just that it was apparent to all that something fulfilling and exciting had happened to us, and that irritated some people.

One day the spiritual leader on campus confronted me. He was thirty-five; I was twenty-one. He was six-foot-seven; I was five-foot-seven. He weighed in at about eighteen stone; I tipped the scales at nine and a half. Thank God the confrontation was verbal and not physical.

So this guy scowled down at me and growled, 'Larry, if you lay your hands on and pray for anybody else, I'm gonna pray that God will chop your arms off right at the elbows.'

The Lord gave me grace and I was able to reach up, put my hand on his shoulder and say, 'I understand why you feel like that, but can't we be brothers?' Yet as I walked away, thoughts about what I could have said and should have said flooded my mind. My tranquil little river of peace boiled into scalding steam. Boy, was I mad. (Actually, I told myself I was just hurt. That's a nice word for angry.)

So I did what you should never do if you want to get over an offence. (I'll borrow five rhyming words from Marilyn Hickey to describe the process.) First, I *cursed* it. I muttered to myself, 'Where does this guy get off, talking to me like that? Who does he think he is, anyway? Get him, God!'

I didn't yet know God sometimes allows offences to help us grow and mature, so my next step wasn't any better. I *nursed* it. I let that ugly little offence curl up in my lap and become my bosom buddy. I coddled it, petted it, fed it. And, sure enough, it grew.

Then I *rehearsed* it. I enjoyed full-colour, slow-motion instant replays of the offence in my mind. Oh, yes, I even edited it to make myself look better, magnifying the injury I had suffered.

But when I finally got tired of reruns and was ready to get on with life, I had this full-grown offence following me around. Ignoring it didn't do any good. Trying to push it away from my mind's threshold didn't work. How was I supposed to get rid of this loathsome thing?

Finally, I found the solution. I *dispersed* it. I gave it to God. I confessed it and forsook it. I humbled myself before God and sought his forgiveness, cleansing and strength.

And then, do you know what God did? He *reversed* it! He turned it around, and the thing that could have become my tombstone became instead a stepping-stone to victory and maturity.

Romans 4:25 (KJV) tells us that Jesus 'was delivered [over to death] for our offences' — not just for the offences of others against us, but for all our offences against him. Forgiveness is what Calvary is all about. Therefore, 'Be kind and compassionate to one another, forgiving each other, just as in Christ God forgave you' (Ephesians 4:32).

When you forgive, you release into God's hands the person who has offended you. You drop the offence, let it go, and give up your right to hurt the person who has hurt you. Then you become a candidate for the supernatural. The peace of God that passes all understanding guards your mind, and God himself, in his own time and in his own way, vindicates you.

his own time and in his own way, vindicates you.

Years ago I served under a church staff member who seemed 'out to get me'. He kept a critical eye cocked in my direction for over a year and did everything he could to make me look bad.

One morning in the staff meeting he said, 'We don't have cheats on our church staff.' Then he glared at me and barked, 'Larry, stand up.'

Wondering what on earth he was about to do, I slowly stood to my feet.

Turning to our fellow-staff members he announced, 'The other night several of us from the church went out to eat, and Larry left without paying his bill. I'll have you know that we're not gonna have people on this staff who walk out of restaurants without paying for their meals.'

I could feel my heart pounding. I struggled to keep my composure. I hadn't left without paying. A businessman from the church had whispered in my ear, 'I know you're late for your television taping so go on ahead. I want to pay for your meal.' I had thanked him and left.

I was completely innocent of this man's accusations. But I had been praying, praising and flowing in the river of the Spirit that morning, and the Holy Spirit would not let me open my mouth. So I just stood there quietly until the man felt he had made his point and told me to sit down. Then when the meeting was dismissed I went to my office and prayed it through, forgiving and releasing the man to God.

Before long, word of this embarrassing incident got around to the man who had paid my bill. (Ironically, he was twice as big and mean as I was.) He stormed into that staff member's office and let him know in no uncertain terms exactly what had happened at the restaurant.

Five minutes later the staff member, his face as white as a sheet, was in my office apologising. I him because I had chosen days before to forgive him and release him to God.

When I took that step, I became a candidate for the supernatural, and God came to my defence just as he promised to do: 'Don't be afraid of those who threaten you. For the time is coming when the truth will be revealed: their secret plots will become public information' (Matthew 10:26 Living Bible).

Isaiah 26:3 pledges, 'You will keep in perfect peace him whose mind is steadfast, because he trusts in you.' That word 'steadfast' actually means 'sustained', 'supported by'. Don't fret about the offence. Lean on, rely on and be confident in him, and he will come to your aid, help you to stand and comfort you.

At this very moment the Spirit of God is defying the spirit of anger, revenge and unforgiveness that has ruled in your life. You can continue to curse, nurse and rehearse the offence, or you can disperse the thing right now in prayer and allow God to reverse it. Remember, you must choose to forgive, for forgiveness is not an emotion but an act of the will.

You have a choice to make about this test that God has allowed to come your way. Will your reaction to the offence fashion it into a tombstone or a stepping-stone?

It's your decision. Make it count!

Review questions

1. Below are statements concerning forgiveness. If a statement is true, write 'T' in the blank provided. If it is false, write 'F'

a. _____ God uses those who sin against us to teach us how to forgive

b. _____ Forgiveness is an important key to spiritual victory, freedom and joy

c. _____ An attitude of unforgiveness is a reason for unanswered prayer

d. _____ When John tells us to confess our sin (1 John 1:9), he is saying we must agree with what God says about our sin and be willing to turn away from it

e. _____ Jesus told Peter to forgive a brother who sinned against him, but no more than seven times

f. _____ Your debt of sin against God is greater than any debt an offender will ever owe you

g. _____ When we refuse to forgive a person, we put that individual in bondage

h. _____ If we do not forgive, God will turn us over to tormentors until we choose to forgive

2. Summarise on the lines below what you are to do daily in order to maintain a forgiving attitude

   _____

   _____

   _____

3. What do you think this statement means: 'Forgiveness is not an emotion. It is an act of the will'?

   _____

   _____

   _____

   _____

   _____

Prayer outline

1. Ask God to forgive you

a. Deal with your sins. Ask the Holy Spirit to reveal areas in your life that are not pleasing to God

b. Confess your sin. Agree with God and say what he says about your sin. Ask him to help you hate your sin with perfect hatred and to deliver you from its dominion. Praise his name, *Jehovah-m'kaddesh*, 'the Lord Who Sanctifies'

c. Do not allow condemnation. Remember: you are the righteousness of God in Christ. You are complete in him

2. Forgive as often as you want to be forgiven

a. Meditate upon your great debt of sin that God has forgiven

b. See your sin actually causing Jesus' suffering on the cross. Get a mental picture of the blood shed for your forgiveness

c. By an act of your will, forgive those who have sinned against you and release them to God. Pray for those who have wronged you

3. Set your will to forgive anyone who sins against you this day

a. Make up your mind to return good for evil by the grace and power of the Holy Spirit within you

b. Make this faith declaration: 'I will love my enemies. I will bless those who curse me and do good to those who hate me. I will pray for those who persecute me (see Matthew 5:44)

c. Pray that you will begin to experience the fruit of the Spirit in your life in greater measure: love, joy, peace, patience, kindness, goodness, faithfulness, gentleness and self-control (Galatians 5:22-23)

Part Six

Power

*'Lead us not into temptation,
but deliver us from the evil one'*

15

Putting on God's armour

What a time to have a heart attack! Unfortunately, Pastor Conatser didn't have any say in the matter.

Although Beverly Hills Baptist Church was exploding with growth, and the only other preaching pastor on his staff was a twenty-two-year-old kid fresh out of Bible college, Pastor Conatser had orders to rest for at least six weeks and let someone else do the preaching. That someone else turned out to be me — the twenty-two-year-old preacher boy.

When the board turned to me and said, 'Larry, it's up to you,' the pressure was awesome. Overnight my responsibilities doubled, and so did my anxieties and frustrations. It wasn't long before a little black cloud of depression followed me around raining gloom and misery on my bedraggled spirit.

But one day a Lutheran pastor visited my study, and he wasn't long in coming to the point. 'Do you put on the whole armour of God every day?' he asked bluntly.

I was a Bible college graduate with three years of Greek recorded on my certificate, so I wanted to impress this pastor and let him know I was no dummy. 'Oh, yes!' I exclaimed, leaning back in my chair and folding my arms across my chest. 'You're referring to that beautiful Pauline metaphor in the sixth chapter of Ephesians. Yes, sir, I'm familiar with its every participle, verb and noun, because I exegeted that entire book from the Greek.'

I knew immediately that he wasn't impressed. 'I'm not asking if you know *about* the armour of God,' he explained patiently. 'I'm asking if you *put on* the whole armour of God every day.'

Somewhat deflated, I shook my head and admitted meekly, 'No sir, I don't.'

The pastor's insightful reply startled me. 'Then maybe that's why you're depressed all the time.'

The whole armour of God

After he left, I took another look at Ephesians 6:10-18, and, phrase by phrase, topic by topic, I studied those nine verses for clues to their relevance for twentieth-century Christians. Would you like to join me in a simplified line-by-line account of what I found?

'Be strong in the Lord, and in his mighty power'
The Christian preparing for conflict needs power. Even if you are fully clad in the armour Paul describes in the verses that follow, you must first have power or the armour is of little benefit. Where do we get that power? Through fellowship with the Lord and in answer to prayer.

'Put on the full armour of God'
As a Christian warrior you are to put on the complete equipment provided, undervaluing nothing, omitting nothing, for how can you know at what unguarded point the enemy may attack?

'So that you can take your stand'
Paul explains that the warrior puts on the whole armour in order to stand. This is a military term that refers to 'the firm and prepared attitude of a good soldier confronting his enemy'.

'Against the devil's schemes'
What is the warrior to stand against? The schemes or stratagems of the devil — the subtle, dangerous ways that evil assails.

'For our struggle is not against flesh and blood, but against the rulers, against the authorities, against the powers of this

dark world and against the spiritual forces of evil in the heavenly realms'
We don't wrestle against visible physical opponents, but against principalities, against the organised forces of evil powers. We wrestle against rulers whose sway over the moral darkness pervading humanity is worldwide. We wrestle against spiritual hosts of wickedness — spiritual cavalry, robber hordes — in all spheres and relations and in the atmosphere around us.

'Therefore put on the full armour of God, so that when the day of evil comes, you may be able to stand your ground'
We are not to rely merely upon human precautions and defences but are to take up the whole armour of God that we may be able to stand against the day of temptation — that special season and circumstance of spiritual or moral testing which may come at any time, and for which it is always necessary to be prepared.

'And after you have done everything, to stand. Stand firm then'
Being in condition for warring a good fight — having done all — we are to stand, intending to conquer.

'With the belt of truth buckled round your waist'
The waist is that part of the body between the ribs and the hip-bones. The digestive system, the reproductive organs and the bowels (which eliminate waste) are contained here.

The leather girdle or apron about the waist of the Roman soldier was the first and most necessary part of his equipment. It not only served to keep the armour in its proper place; it was also used to support the sword.

Paul teaches that our waist is to be buckled around with truth — inward truth, genuineness and determined purpose. The psalmist said, 'Surely you desire truth in the inner parts; you teach me wisdom in the inmost place' (Psalm 51:6).

As a believer, you are to be filled with the truth of God; you are to be a person of total integrity and moral rectitude. You must know who you are in God and who God is in you. You buckle the belt of truth around your waist by reaffirming the truth about yourself and about God and by acting upon that truth instead of upon your emotions.

'With the breastplate of righteousness in place'
The breastplate was a piece of armour worn over the chest. Organs vital to life itself were protected by the breastplate: the oesophagus (the passage for food from the mouth to the stomach), the windpipe, the heart and the lungs.

What is the believer's breastplate of righteousness? It is the righteousness of God through faith. It is justification by the blood of the cross. This righteousness is the result of the renovation of the heart by the Holy Spirit.

The breastplate is an important part of the soldier's defensive armour. The righteous new man within the believer resists, defends against and refuses to entertain evil suggestions. The breastplate of righteousness diligently guards the heart of the believer, for out of the heart are the issues of life.

'And with your feet fitted with the readiness that comes from the gospel of peace'
In hand-to-hand combat, the ability to stand, side-step, walk and run is absolutely essential. Because a Roman soldier's fighting was mostly hand to hand, a firm footing was extremely important. His sandals were not only bound firmly to his feet and ankles, but the soles were thickly studded with hobnails or spikes to prevent the warrior from slipping.

As participants in spiritual warfare, we are to equip

our feet with the the readiness and preparedness, the firm-footed stability, found in the gospel of peace. As we walk daily in the revealed will of God and order our conduct and conversation according to his Word, we will experience a sense of oneness with God and a consciousness of divine aid equal to any problem.

As believers, we are to walk in the will of God and, as my missionary friend Alice Huff says, leave 'footprints of peace' wherever we go.

'In addition to all this, take up the shield of faith'
The shield was a piece of armour carried on the arm or in the hand to protect and cover the entire body in battle. It was a part of the soldier's armament that could be shifted about and lifted up over all parts of the body as needed.

As Christian believers, our faith serves us just as a shield serves the soldier, but how do we get faith? Ephesians 2:8-9 says that faith is a gift. Romans 10:17 says, 'Faith comes from hearing the message, and the message is heard through the word *[rhema]* of Christ.' Galatians 5:22-23 says that faith is part of the fruit of the Holy Spirit. Galatians 2:20 says we live by the faith of the Son of God, who loved us and gave himself for us. That faith is the believer's shield.

'With which you can extinguish all the flaming arrows of the evil one'
'The evil one' does not refer to an impersonal force, but to Satan and the evil foes described in verse 12.

The large shields of ancient soldiers were made of wood (so they would be lightweight) and were covered with hides. The hides were soaked in water to quench flaming arrows, the enemy's most dangerous missiles shot to destroy and wound mortally. Paul assures us that 'the shield of faith' will prevail against Satan's worst forms of attack.

The believer takes the shield of faith and declares,

'I'm trusting in you, Lord, to protect me. Because I'm hiding in you, nothing can touch me today that you do not allow.'

'Take the helmet of salvation'
The helmet, the most expensive piece of the armour, was worn to protect the head. The helmet of salvation protects the believer's mind and thinking.

The word 'take' in this verse literally means 'receive' — to take in hand the helmet of salvation, which is 'the gift of God'. Therefore, the believer is consciously to ask for and receive the mind of Christ and the peace of God that garrisons and mounts guard over his thoughts (see Philippians 4:7 Amp).

'And the sword of the Spirit, which is the word of God'
The sword was an offensive weapon with a sharp blade fixed in a handle or hilt. Used to wound or kill, the sword was a symbol of power or authority, especially to judge and impose sentence.

The Christian's power and authority are the word of God. In speaking of the sword of the Spirit or the word of God, the reference here is not to *logos* or the whole Bible as such, but to *rhema* — the individual scripture, statement, command or instruction which the Spirit speaks to our spirits or brings to our remembrance for use in time of need. Before we are able to wield the sword of the Spirit effectively, we must fill our minds with Scripture.

The Greek indicates that the believer must receive this specific word from God for a specific situation. The special revelation can then be used as a sharp sword against the enemy and his onslaughts.

'And pray in the Spirit on all occasions with all kinds of prayers and requests'
The last powerful piece of the whole armour of God is *praying always in the Spirit*. This means praying in

tongues, praying in and with your spirit in your own personal prayer language inspired by the Holy Spirit (Acts 2:4; 1 Corinthians 14:2, 14-15; Jude 20).

Because you are not praying with your mind but with your spirit, it is possible to obey Paul's command to 'pray in the Spirit on all occasions' (Ephesians 6:18). The only way you can pray on all occasions — or continually (1 Thessalonians 5:17) — is to pray with your spirit.

Your mind is limited; it hinders you from praying as you ought. But your spirit, redeemed by the blood and filled with the Holy Spirit of God, is unlimited. As you pray, the Spirit comes to your aid, joins his strong supplication with yours and intercedes before God on your behalf and for the welfare of other believers. As the Holy Spirit enables you to pray according to the perfect will of God, your prayers get through (Romans 8:26-27).

Consider this: your spirit has instant access to your vocal cords just as your mind has. Therefore, by your will, a prayer in your prayer language can come out of your spirit, bypass your mind, go over your tongue and go straight to God. God's response to your prayer can then be registered in your mind, enabling you to pray with understanding (1 Corinthians 14:13-15).

Have you ever groped for words, sensing the weaknesses and limitations of your own mind and understanding as you poured out your heart to God? Have you ever been caught in tense, urgent situations where there was no time to slip away by yourself and pray?

I have. That is why this seventh piece of spiritual armour is so precious to me. I can use it like a laser beam to pierce right through the devil's territory, reach God and receive his immediate response back to my mind. I can live in a constant attitude of prayer, regardless of where I am or what I am doing. I can pray aloud or under my breath; I can pray alone or

in the middle of a crowd. God knows. God hears. And
God answers. This is how the armour-clad believer
can maintain a prayerful frame of mind and pray at
all times, on all occasions.

'With this in mind, be alert'
This refers to the care the believer is to take not to
neglect the prayer so essential for victory in spiritual
conflicts.

'And always keep on praying for all the saints'
No soldier should pray for himself alone, but for all
his fellow-soldiers also, for they form one army. The
success of one is the success of all.

When Jesus commands believers to pray, 'Lead us
not into temptation,' he is instructing us to pray that
forces beyond our own control will not lead us into
trials. He is commanding us to watch and pray against
entering into temptation through our own carelessness
or disobedience.

The petition 'Deliver us from the evil one' goes
beyond the sense of a test or trial related to our
inclination to sin. It introduces the supplication to be
saved from the grasping, potent power of evil that
seeks to influence, overcome and master us, then lead
us astray. This request involves much more than
merely asking to overcome a desire to sin; we must
also defeat the powerful, evil forces seeking to hinder
or destroy God's plan for our lives.

Therefore, in Ephesians 6:11, 13, Paul instructs us
to put on the whole armour of God so that we will be
able to stand against the schemes of the devil.

What is the obvious reverse of this teaching? If we
do not pray, 'Lead us not into temptation, but deliver
us from the evil one,' if we do not put on the whole
armour of God, we cannot stand against the schemes
of the devil. We will not stand!

In Romans Paul again mentions the armour. There

he instructs us to put on 'the armour of light' and to clothe ourselves 'with the Lord Jesus Christ' (Romans 13:12, 14).

The armour Paul describes and commands the believer to put on is really the Lord Jesus Christ. Jesus wants to be our defence and to clothe us with himself.

How to put on the armour

As I learned from the Lutheran pastor, this passage in Ephesians was not written just to be a beautiful metaphor. It was written to be obeyed and applied in everyday life.

But how does a believer put on armour he or she cannot see, touch or feel? By faith, visualising each piece. We put on our armour by believing and confessing God's promises. Each day, the believer should pray Ephesians 6:14-17 and in faith put on the whole armour of God, piece by piece. Take a minute to learn how to put on the armour of light, the Lord Jesus Christ.

Armour	Declaration	Promise
The belt of *truth*	Jesus is my truth.	'I am the way and the truth and the life' (John 14:6). 'You teach me wisdom in the inmost place' (Psalm 51:6)
Breastplate of *righteousness*	Jesus, you are my righteousness	'God made him who had no sin to be sin for us, so that in him we might become the righteousness of God' (2 Corinthians 5:21). 'You have been given fulness in Christ' (Colossians 2:10)
Feet fitted with the *readiness* of the gospel of peace	Jesus, you are my readiness	'I can do everything through him who gives me strength' (Philippians 4:13)

The shield of *faith*	Jesus, you are my faith	'I have been crucified with Christ and I no longer live, but Christ lives in me. The life I live in the body, I live by faith in the Son of God, who loved me and gave himself for me' (Galatians 2:20). 'Faith comes from hearing the message, and the message is heard through the word *[rhema]* of Christ' (Romans 10:17)
The helmet of *salvation*	Jesus, you are my salvation	'Once made perfect, he became the source of eternal salvation for all who obey him' (Hebrews 5:9). 'O Sovereign Lord, my strong deliverer, who shields my head in the day of battle' (Psalm 140:7)
Sword of the *Spirit* which is the word *(rhema)* of God	Jesus, you are my living word	'The words *[rhema]* I have spoken to you are spirit and they are life' (John 6:63)
Praying in the Spirit on all occasions	Jesus, you are my baptiser in the Spirit	'He will baptise you with the Holy Spirit and with fire' (Matthew 3:11). 'He who searches the hearts of men knows what is in the mind of the (Holy) Spirit – what his intent is – because the Spirit intercedes and pleads [before God] on behalf of the saints according to and in harmony with God's will' (Romans 8:27 Amp).

For many years now, I have daily put on the whole armour of God, piece by piece, by believing and declaring God's promises.

How about you? You wouldn't dream of going to work or to church without dressing properly, but day after day are you walking around without your spiritual clothes on? Are you a spiritual 'streaker'? If so, the devil sees you walking around spiritually naked, and he laughs because he knows you are defenceless against his schemes.

Learn to put on the whole armour of God, and do it every day. Refuse to let Satan delay or destroy God's purpose for your life. And pray a hedge of protection around yourself and your loved ones. That's what we learn to do next.

16

Building a hedge of protection

When I was a kid, I never sat in the dust with two puffy eyes and a bloodied nose exclaiming, 'Boy, that was a good fight.'

It wasn't a good fight unless I won!

Then why does Paul call our war with Satan a 'good' fight (1 Timothy 6:12)? It is identified as a good fight because we are supposed to win. We win by praying, 'Lead us not into temptation, but deliver us from the evil one.' We win by putting on the whole armour of God and by building the hedge of protection around ourselves.

Are you tired of eating the devil's dust? Would you like to know how to flatten the dude and plant your hobnail boots on his greedy throat? Then you must prepare yourself to stand in the victory Jesus has already won for you by putting on the whole armour of God and by learning to build a hedge of protection.

Build a hedge of protection

Build a hedge of protection about yourself and your loved ones daily by your faith declaration from Psalm 91:2: 'I will say of the Lord, "He is my refuge and my fortress, my God, in whom I trust."' In the Amplified Bible, the next verse states: 'For [then] he will deliver you from the snare of the fowler.'

Later in the chapter (v9, 14 Amp) are three reasons — or 'becauses' — why you can claim God's protection: 'Because you have made the Lord your refuge, and the Most High your dwelling-place'; 'Because he has set his love upon me'; and 'Because he knows and understands my name'.

Because we have made the Lord our dwelling
As we believers sing praises to the Lord, he sits down
among us, enthroned upon our praises. Psalm 22:3
(RAV) states: 'You are holy, who inhabit [sit down
or dwell among] the praises *[tehillah* — songs, psalms,
the residing song of the Spirit] of Israel.'

Because Paul knew this secret, he instructed: 'Do
not get drunk on wine, which leads to debauchery.
Instead, be filled with the Spirit. Speak to one another
with psalms, hymns and spiritual songs. Sing and
make music in your heart to the Lord' (Ephesians
5:18-19).

In another passage, Paul, an example to believers,
said he sang with the spirit and also with the
understanding (1 Corinthians 14:15). You, too, are to
sing to the Lord in praise and worship. At times, you
will enjoy singing beautiful old hymns or choruses. At
other times, you may feel like making up your own
special songs and singing them to the Lord. And
sometimes, the Holy Spirit may compose a spon-
taneous song of praise in a language only God's ears
and your own heart understand.

As you sing to God, he inhabits your praises. That
is how you make the Lord your habitation or dwelling.
As you walk with him in the Spirit, he will be your
refuge.

Because we have set our love upon him
We can also claim God's protection if we set our love
upon him. We set our love upon the Lord by focusing
our affections upon him, by seeking him first.

David declared: 'One thing I ask of the Lord, this
is what I seek: that I may dwell in the house of the
Lord all the days of my life, to gaze upon the beauty
of the Lord and to seek him in his temple. *For in the
day of trouble* he will keep me safe in his *dwelling;* he
will hide me in the shelter of his tabernacle and set

me high upon a rock. Then my head will be exalted above the enemies who surround me; at his tabernacle will I sacrifice with shouts of joy; *I will sing and make music to the Lord'* (Psalm 27:4-6).

The word 'dwelling' in verse 5 means 'a temporary, movable tent, or a more permanent building'. During war, the royal dwelling — the king's tent — was erected in the centre of his army, and it was surrounded by a constant guard of mighty men.

David, a king who occupied one of those royal tents in battle, is saying: 'In the time of trouble, God hides me in his royal tent in the very centre of his army, and surrounds me by a constant guard of angels.' In Psalm 91:10-11 we are assured, 'No disaster will come near your tent. For he will command his angels concerning you to guard you in all your ways.' And Psalm 34:7 declares, 'The angel of the Lord encamps around those who fear him, and he delivers them.'

If we want to be surrounded by God's hedge of protection, we must set our love upon him. In Psalm 27:4 David declared, 'One thing I ask . . . .' Have you ever noticed other references to the words 'one thing' in Scripture? To the rich young ruler Jesus said, 'You still lack one thing . . .' (Luke 18:22). To Martha he said, 'You are worried and upset about many things, but only one thing is needed . . .' (Luke 10:41-42). Paul declared, 'One thing I do . . .' (Philippians 3:13).

We, like Martha, are often anxious and troubled about many things, but we lack one important thing. We hurry and scurry about, busy with our own business, but we neglect our Father's business.

Here's an example with which you might identify.

When my son was younger and I asked him to mow the lawn, he would sometimes put off the job and play instead. I didn't mind his playing with friends, but his disobedience and his not mowing the lawn disturbed me.

I think it's like that with our heavenly Father. He

says, 'Tarry with me one hour,' but we put our own things first and before we know it, the day is over and we haven't spent time with God. It's time for us to grow up spiritually and learn to give our Father the first hour of our day; then there will be twenty-three more hours to take care of our own things.

We need to allow the Holy Spirit to focus our energies and attentions upon the Lord — to set our love upon him. As we cling to him in absolute trust, he will be our protection.

Because we acknowledge his name
'The name of the Lord is a strong tower; the righteous run to it and are safe' (Proverbs 18:10). The name of the Lord signifies not only who he is, but what he wants to be in your life.

Don't misuse the Lord's name. He is more than saviour. He is your righteousness and sanctifier. He is your peace, and the overflowing one present within you. He is your healer and provider, banner and shepherd. So know his name, for it is a strong tower. Let him be what you need him to be in your life.

Declare God's hedge of protection
Every day, make the Lord your habitation by singing songs of praise. Set your love upon him and seek him first, above all else. Know and submit to his name. Inspect your spirit and make certain you are living in the three 'becauses' of Psalm 91.

Then you can stand in your armour and declare: 'You are my refuge, my fortress, my God. In you do I trust. I know your name. You are my righteousness, sanctifier, peace, healer, provider, banner and shepherd, and your presence dwells within me.'

That is the way to pray a hedge of protection about yourself and your loved ones. When you live in these three 'becauses' and daily declare that he is your refuge and fortress, the Lord's hedge of protection forms around you like a nest around a bird, or a cocoon around a butterfly larva.

I realise that some people laugh at the idea of God's hedge of protection, but the devil doesn't. He knows it's real. Just take a moment to study this complaint Satan made to God about Job: 'Have you not put a hedge about him and his house and all that he has, on every side? You have conferred prosperity and happiness upon him in the work of his hands, and his possessions have increased in the land' (Job 1:10 Amp).

Notice three things God does for his children: he puts a hedge around us, our homes and all that we have on every side; he confers happiness and prosperity (not one or the other) upon us in the work of our hands; he makes our possessions increase, not decrease.

So every day as you pray, 'Lead us not into temptation, but deliver us from the evil one,' declare that hedge of protection around yourself, your friends and loved ones, your home and all that you have. Ask God to confer happiness and prosperity on the work of your hands and to make your possessions — both spiritual and material — increase in the land. Hallelujah!

Clothe yourself in the armour of light — the Lord Jesus Christ — and pray God's encircling hedge of protection around all you hold dear. And having done all, stand . . . . Stand in the victory Jesus Christ has won for you.

Review questions

1. If the following statements are true, write 'T' in the blank; if false, write 'F'.

a. _____ Believers can enter into temptation by their own carelessness and disobedience

b. _____ The armour Paul talks about in Ephesians 6 is actually the armour of light, Jesus Christ

c. _____ If we do not put on the whole armour of God, we will not stand against the devil

2. Why is our war with Satan called a *good* fight?

3. What are the three reasons — or 'becauses' — in Psalm 91:9, 14 that allow you to claim God's protection?

a. _____

b. _____

c. _____

Prayer outline

1. Put on the whole armour of God

a. Belt of truth

b. Breastplate of righteousness

c. Feet shod with the readiness of the gospel of peace

d. Shield of faith

e. Helmet of salvation

f. Sword of the Spirit which is the word of God

g. Praying always in the Spirit

2. Build a hedge of protection

a. Three 'becauses'
   ☐ Because we have made the Lord our dwelling
   ☐ Because we have set our love upon him
   ☐ Because we acknowledge his name

b. Declare: 'He is my refuge and my fortress, my God, in whom I trust'

Part Seven

Praise

'Yours is the kingdom and the power and the glory for ever'

17

Obeying God's most dynamic commandment

As we noted previously, the Lord's Prayer opens and closes with praise.

Praise is the Word's most dynamic commandment. Why do I make that claim? Because regular worship and praise reconstitute God's people — restore us to the spiritual state that God intended — and give believers the dynamic — the supernatural energy and force — so vital to victory, wholeness and harmony. Therefore, we need to learn how to let our hearts go out to God in praise and thanksgiving, magnifying and exalting his perfections and mighty deeds and thanking him for all his benefits.

The Bible states that the unrighteous refuse to offer praise to God (Romans 1:21; Revelation 16:9), but God's people always have been and always will be people of praise. It isn't surprising that the Word of God reveals many ways to express our love, gratitude and worship to the Lord. A survey of the Scriptures shows that we are to praise God with our mouths, through our bodily movements and through the playing and singing of music.

Three Hebrew words in the Old Testament demonstrate how believers are to use their mouths in praising God.

Hallal means 'to be vigorously excited; to laud, boast, rave, to celebrate'. This type of praise is done with a loud voice. *Barak* is 'to bless, to declare God the origin of power for success, prosperity and fertility; to be still'. This praise may be quiet and hushed, while another Hebrew word for praise, *shabach,* means 'to commend, address in a loud tone, to shout'. As we set our hearts to worship God acceptably, the Holy Spirit will teach us how and when to use our mouths in offering praise to God.

Bodily movement is also associated with praise, as we see in two Old Testament words for praise. *Todah* means 'to extend the hands in thanksgiving'. *Yadah* is 'to worship with extended hands — to throw out the hands, enjoying God'.

It is time God's people realised that raising the hands in worship is not a new charismatic fad; rather, it is a scriptural principle. For instance, the psalmist commanded, 'Lift up your hands in the sanctuary and praise the Lord' (Psalm 134:2). Four times Psalm 107 (KJV) urges longingly: 'Oh that men would praise *[yadah]* the Lord for his goodness, and for his wonderful works to the children of men!'

So as you worship God, obey the leading of his Holy Spirit. Don't be afraid to stand, kneel, bow, dance, clap your hands or lift them to the Lord. Each of these forms of praise is perfectly scriptural when done decently and in order.

We are to use not only our mouths and our bodies in worship; we are also to employ music in praise. *Zamar* means 'to pluck the strings of an instrument, to praise with song', and *tehillah* is the word for singing in the Spirit or the singing of hallals or psalms. We can worship God through singing and playing songs of praise.

We must not be afraid to yield to the leading of the Holy Spirit and to let him teach us how to use our mouths, our bodily movements and our music to worship the Lord.

After we have brought our petitions to God our Father, we should return to praise. The words, 'Yours is the kingdom and the power and the glory for ever,' are idle words to most people. Many believers don't realise that God has lovingly invited us to become participants in his kingdom, his power and his glory.

The kingdom

'The kingdom is the Lord's,' declared the psalmist, and Jesus said, 'Yours is the kingdom' (Psalm 22:28 KJV; Matthew 6:13 margin). But Jesus also said, 'Do not be afraid, little flock, for your Father has been pleased to give you the kingdom' (Luke 12:32).

Paul also teaches that we are partakers in God's kingdom: 'Giving thanks to the Father . . . . For he has rescued us from the dominion of darkness and brought us into the kingdom of the Son he loves' (Colossians 1:12-13). To Timothy Paul declared: 'The Lord will rescue me from every evil attack and will bring me safely to his heavenly kingdom. To him be glory for ever and ever' (2 Timothy 4:18).

Therefore, as you pray, 'For yours is the kingdom,' praise God your Father who delivered you from the power of darkness and brought you into his kingdom of love and light. Make the faith declaration: 'The Lord will deliver me from every evil work and preserve me to his heavenly kingdom.' Give God praise because he has invited you to be a participant in his kingdom.

The power

David wrote, 'In your hands are strength and power' (1 Chronicles 29:12), and he declared, 'Be exalted, O Lord, in your strength; we will sing and praise your might' (Psalm 21:13). God made the earth by his power (Jeremiah 10:12) and will rule by his power for ever (Psalm 66:7).

Yet God our Father has made us participants in his power. He gives strength and power to his people (Psalm 68:35) and gives us power to produce wealth (Deuteronomy 8:17-18). He gives power to the weak (Isaiah 40:29) and shields us by his power (1 Peter 1:5). God our Father, who raised up Jesus, will raise us up by his mighty power (1 Corinthians 6:14).

Jesus declared, 'I have given you authority to trample on snakes and scorpions and to overcome all the power of the enemy; nothing will harm you' (Luke 10:19). Just before his ascension, the Lord instructed the disciples: 'I am going to send you what my Father has promised; but stay in the city until you have been clothed with power from on high' (Luke 24:49). In Acts 1:8 we read again the words of Jesus promising the power of the Holy Spirit: 'You will receive power when the Holy Spirit comes on you; and you will be my witnesses in Jerusalem, and in all Judea and Samaria, and to the ends of the earth.'

Paul instructs us to 'be strong in the Lord and in his mighty power' (Ephesians 6:10). And in 1 Corinthians 4:20 he affirms: 'The kingdom of God is not a matter of talk but of power.'

Give praise to God your Father because he has invited you to be a participant in his power and has made his power available to you.

The glory

'Who is this King of glory?' asked the psalmist. 'The Lord strong and mighty, the Lord mighty in battle' (Psalm 24:8). 'Glory and honour are in his presence' (1 Chronicles 16:27 KJV). God himself declares: 'I am the Lord; that is my name! I will not give my glory to another or my praise to idols' (Isaiah 42:8).

What is God's glory? It is the manifested perfection of his character, especially his righteousness. We know all people fall short of God's glory (Romans 3:23), yet he has invited believers to be participants in his glory. Jesus made this possible, as we see in Hebrews 2:9-10. Jesus, in suffering for the sins of humankind, brought many sons to glory.

Paul assured believers that if we suffer with Jesus, we will also be glorified together (Romans 8:17). Suffering was of little consequence to Paul, for he knew that the present sufferings cannot be compared

with the glory which will eventually be revealed in us
(Romans 8:18).

As we behold the glory of the Lord — the character
and ways of God exhibited through Christ — we are
slowly changed into his image by the Spirit of God
(2 Corinthians 3:18), and the character and ways of
the Father and Son are formed within us. Brought into
Christ's likeness, we will enter eternal blessedness, for
God our Father has called us to his eternal glory (1
Peter 5:10).

Is it any wonder that Paul charged believers to 'live
lives worthy of God, who calls you into his kingdom
and glory' (1 Thessalonians 2:11-12)? Give praise to
God because he has invited you to be a participant in
his glory.

David urges believers to witness to others of God's
kingdom, power and glory: 'All you have made will
praise you, O Lord; your saints will extol you. They
will tell of the glory of your kingdom and speak of your
might, so that all men may know of your mighty acts
and the glorious splendour of your kingdom. Your
kingdom is an everlasting kingdom, and your
dominion endures through all generations' (Psalm
145:10-13).

We praise you, Father, for yours is the kingdom and
the power and the glory for ever, yet you have invited
us to become participants. May we never enter or
leave your presence without humbly bowing before
you and offering a sacrifice of praise.

May we proclaim with David: 'Praise be to you,
O Lord, God of our father Israel, from everlasting to
everlasting. Yours, O Lord, is the greatness and the
power and the glory and the majesty and the
splendour, for everything in heaven and earth is yours.
Yours, O Lord, is the kingdom; you are exalted as
head over all. Wealth and honour come from you; you
are the ruler of all things. In your hands are strength
and power to exalt and give strength to all. Now, our

God, we give you thanks, and praise your glorious
name' (1 Chronicles 29:10-13).

Review questions

1. _____ is the Word's most dynamic commandment

2. Hebrews 13:15 states: 'Through Jesus . . . let us continually offer
   to God a sacrifice of _____ — the fruit of lips that confess his
   name'

3. The Lord's Prayer opens and closes with _____
   _____

4. God has made provision for us to share in his kingdom, power
   and glory. That provision is _____
   _____

5. Now that you know how and what to pray, will you ask the Holy
   Spirit to transform you heart into a house of prayer? If so, why
   not put that desire into words in the space provided below?

   _____

   _____

   _____

Prayer outline

1. The kingdom
a. Praise the Lord because he has transferred you from the kingdom
   of darkness to the kingdom of love and light
b. Make the faith declaration: 'The Lord will preserve me from
   every evil work, and preserve me to his heavenly kingdom'
c. Praise God because he has invited you to be a participant in his
   kingdom

2. The power
a. Praise the Lord because he has invited you to be a participant
   in his power
b. Meditate on the power of God your Father. Measure your
   problems against his mighty, miraculous works and his great love
   for you

c. Make this faith declaration: 'I am strong in the Lord and in the power of his might. I have been endued with power from on high. Greater is he who is in me than he who is in the world. My Father gives me strength and power to obtain wealth. He gives power to the weak. As my day so shall my strength be. He keeps me by his power. He has given me power to tread upon serpents and scorpions, and over all the power of the enemy. Nothing will hurt me'

3. The glory

a. Behold the glory of the Lord — the character and ways of God exhibited through Christ. Ask the Holy Spirit to change you into the same image by forming Christ within you. Ask that you be transformed by the renewing of your mind

b. Ask the Lord to help you walk worthy of him and to help you serve him as he deserves to be served

c. Praise him and give him glory

Part Eight

Prerequisites, patterns, participation

18

Putting first things first

The years 1972 to 1978 were a struggle for Melva and me, as we frantically juggled unbalanced priorities and impossible schedules.

As if the thousand young people in our youth group at Beverly Hills Baptist Church were not enough to keep us busy, Melva drove about forty miles each way to work on her master's degree at North Texas State University in Denton, while I drove almost forty miles to Southwestern Baptist Theological Seminary in Forth Worth to complete my master's.

It was during those years that our three children were born in rapid succession. Our friends probably referred to my wife as 'Melva the saint'. She was amazing. But I wasn't measuring up to the man of God that I wanted to be.

What troubled me? The anointed presence of God seemed to be receding in my life. Why? Because I wasn't rising early day by day, worshipping my Father, praying and receiving from him what I needed.

I wasn't beginning each day by entering God's presence with thanksgiving and his courts with praise. I was carelessly neglecting God's exceedingly great and precious promises by which we are partakers of the divine nature (see 2 Peter 1:4). I wasn't always allowing him to be my righteousness, sanctifier, peace, healer, provider, banner, shepherd and the overflowing present one within me. Therefore, I often took his names in vain.

Because I didn't set the rudder of my life (my tongue) upon God's priorities for my life by daily declaring,

'Your kingdom come, your will be done in me, my family, my church and my nation,' my priorities seemed to be upside down much of the time. Money was tight, so we barely scraped by every month. We tithed and gave offerings, but because I wasn't specifically, tenaciously praying every day, 'Give us today our daily bread,' we weren't prospering in many areas.

Furthermore, because of my faults and failures, I also had a problem from time to time with feeling 'accepted in the Beloved' (Ephesians 1:6 RAV). I continually asked God to forgive me for things of which I had repented long before, forgetting that I was purged from my old sins (2 Peter 1:9). I sometimes had the notion that I was on probation with God and that someday, if I became good enough, he would accept me.

For years I did 'Protestant Penance'. In the Roman Catholic Church you do penance by repeating a prescribed act a certain number of times to show sorrow for sin and to get yourself to the place where you feel forgiven. But in protestant churches, we don't do that. (You see, we're more 'spiritual'.) Instead, when we do something wrong, we spend two weeks, or two decades, kicking ourselves. Am I right? That's 'Protestant Penance'. But actually God freely forgave us the moment we confessed our failure to him.

I didn't rise every morning and say: 'I confess every known sin to you, Lord, even the ones I don't know I've committed. I accept that you have forgiven me, and I also set my will to forgive those who sin against me.' Therefore, it took a long time for the truth to dawn on me: by begging over and over for God to forgive a particular sin or failure, I was remembering what God had forgotten.

I fought battles with fear and depression, but for most of the time I lost. How could I expect to win against a wily, well-armed foe when I wore no armour and didn't know how to wield effectively the sword of the Spirit or skilfully employ the shield of faith to ward off his ruthless attacks?

How could I fight the good fight of faith when I didn't pray in my prayer language daily and live in an attitude of prayer?

Praise didn't continually flow out of my spirit to God. I didn't know that I could put on the garment of praise *(tehillah)* instead of the spirit of heaviness by singing songs of praise to God (Isaiah 61:3).

And the truth hadn't yet registered in my spirit that God my Father has made me a participant in his kingdom, power and glory.

But since 1978, when the Holy Spirit revealed to me that the Lord's Prayer is a prayer outline, I have entered into the presence of Jesus every day. And what have I received in return?

Promises

Each day of my life I thank God that, because of the blood of Jesus, I can call him Father. I praise his glorious names, appropriate his mighty promises and seek to sanctify his name through my manner of living.

Priorities

Although I am busier now than ever before, I enjoy peace inside me, in my home and in my church. Why? Because I pray daily over myself, my family, my church and my nation, declaring that God's priorities in those areas be set in order. I boldly declare that God's righteousness, joy and peace shall come and that his will shall be done.

Provision

No longer am I the anxiety-ridden victim of frustrating circumstances. Instead, I am learning to experience the abundant provision of *Jehovah-jireh*, the one who sees our needs ahead of time and makes provision for them, because I don't take God's blessings for granted.

Every day in prayer, I set my will to make God's kingdom my priority. Then I pray through on my needs, claiming and receiving God's promised provision, and each day he gives me my daily bread. You, too, can experience more and more freedom from frustration by setting your priorities straight.

If daily bread is a constant struggle for you, don't be anxious and fret about it. God gave me a personal promise that you, too, can claim: 'The day you answer the call to pray, I will begin to meet your needs.'

People

If you are plagued by guilt or problems with people, remember, you must forgive. That doesn't just happen automatically. Every day we need to forgive our debtors before we can receive God's washing and cleansing, and then set our wills to forgive those who may wrong us that day. As we learn to forgive and release our offenders and offences to God, we become candidates for the supernatural.

Power

If you want to stop letting the devil push you around, if you want to leave him sitting in the dust for a change, you must learn to put on the whole armour of God each day and to pray a hedge of protection around yourself, your loved ones and all you have. Learn to overcome Satan in the place of prayer by the blood of the Lamb and by the word of your testimony because, if you don't, *you* will be overcome.

These are some of the benefits that have come to me since I learned to give priority to prayer in my daily life. These benefits can be yours as well. The Word of God makes it unmistakably plain. If we are to take our places as participants in God's kingdom, power and glory, we must answer the call to pray.

Think about this: if Jesus needed to pray every day,

how much more must we!

In order to document the importance of prayer in the life of our Lord, I want you to stop for just a moment and meditate with me on one day in his life. Mark, in the first chapter of his gospel, records such a day.

After walking along the shore of the Sea of Galilee and calling Peter, Andrew, James and John to follow him and become fishers of men, Jesus went to the synagogue at Capernaum. There he taught the people, concluding his message by casting an unclean spirit out of a man who had disrupted the service.

Then he went to the home of Peter and Andrew and healed Simon Peter's mother-in-law of a fever. That evening when the sun set, the whole city gathered at the door of Peter's home. They had brought to Jesus everyone who was sick or possessed with demons, and he healed them.

Can you imagine how exhausted Jesus must have been when he finally hit the pillow late that night and drifted off to sleep? But look at the next verse, Mark 1:35: 'Very early in the morning, while it was still dark, Jesus got up, left the house and went off to a solitary place, where he prayed.'

That pattern continued throughout Christ's ministry. Indeed, at the place of prayer Jesus found the power and guidance he needed to fulfil his Father's will each day. He was the Son of God, yet he prayed. Jesus was the busiest, most important man who ever walked the face of this earth, yet prayer was the primary focus of his life.

Isn't it time that you made an agreement with the Lord to meet him every day at the place of prayer?

If you choose an early morning hour, set your clock. When the alarm goes off, don't turn it off, roll over and mumble all the reasons why you need more rest. If you do that, within a few days you won't even hear the alarm. Instead, when it's time to pray, roll out of bed and get dressed. If drinking your morning coffee or having breakfast before you pray will help you wake up and concentrate on what you're doing, then those extra minutes in the kitchen will be well spent.

To develop an effective prayer life, you must overcome these three enemies of prayer: interruptions, drowsiness and wandering thoughts. Let's learn right now how to attack and defeat these enemies.

Interruptions

The telephone and the doorbell can become dire enemies of the believer who seeks to make a discipline of prayer. That is why many busy people choose to pray early in the morning before these distractions begin.

The psalmist David had neither a telephone nor a doorbell, but he did have at least eight wives, ten concubines, twenty-two kids and a kingdom to run. It isn't surprising, then, that one of David's prayer times was early in the morning. David said: 'O Lord, in the morning you hear my voice; in the morning I lay my requests before you and wait in expectation' (Psalm 5:3).

On the other hand, Susannah Wesley, the mother of nineteen children (two of whom were John and Charles who founded the Methodist movement), chose from one to two o'clock each day for her time with the Lord. Every day at one o'clock in the afternoon, Susannah Wesley closed her bedroom door, knelt beside her bed, spread her open Bible before her and talked with God.

Think of it! There were no supermarkets, primary schools, department stores, fast food restaurants, washing-machines and tumble-dryers or modern-day kitchen appliances in Susannah's time. This woman, who was also a preacher's wife, had to make the family's clothes and wash them by hand, clean up after, cook for and home-school all those children, yet she made time every day for an hour with God. How would you like to try to explain to Susannah Wesley why you can't find time to pray?

You may be saying, 'Larry, an early morning prayer time simply won't work for me.'

I understand. Many people, ministers included, don't get to bed before midnight. I'm not trying to induce you to choose an early morning hour to pray, even though that might work best for me. There's nothing 'holy' about four in the morning. What is important is that you choose the time best for you and begin praying an hour every day.

Learn to flow with the Holy Spirit. For instance, your clock may be set for five-thirty in the morning, but the Holy Spirit of God may awaken you at three-thirty and say, 'It's time to pray.' Or your usual prayer time might be eight in the evening. If at six-thirty that evening you sense the Spirit of God stirring your spirit and calling you to prayer, obey his prompting. Don't be bound to a clock; instead, be obedient to the Spirit.

You see, prayer isn't just an hour a day. An hour a day is important only if it develops in us an attitude of prayer for the whole day. Jesus moved and ministered in a spirit of prayer because prayer occupied a much greater place in his life and ministry than just one solitary hour before dawn.

That's what must happen in our lives if we are to become victorious warriors instead of weary worshippers. Paul summed it up for us when he said, 'In him we live and move and have our being' (Acts 17:28). That's it, my friend. That's the secret. God help us not to settle for anything less.

Whether you choose morning, midday or evening as your prayer time, it is important that you have a set *time* and *place* to pray.

Jesus, in teaching his disciples to pray, instructed: 'When you pray, go into your room, close the door and pray to your Father, who is unseen' (Matthew 6:6).

That means that you need to choose a quiet, private place to pray and meet God every day. It doesn't have to be a fancy place; just a chair beside which you can kneel will do. But having a set time and place to pray will help defeat those interruptions.

Drowsiness

How can believers defeat the enemy of drowsiness when they pray? Some of John Wesley's early Methodist leaders who were determined to overcome this problem actually soaked towels in cold water, wrapped them around their heads and went right on praying! That's not the method I would choose, but I certainly admire their tenacity.

If you find yourself dropping off to sleep every time you kneel, cradling your head on your arm and closing your eyes to pray, why not try sitting or standing? Or why not try *walking* as you pray? Move a chair or table out of the way and walk back and forth across a room, or pace up and down a hall. You will quickly grow accustomed to the 'path'. Then you will be able to concentrate solely on prayer and defeat the enemy of drowsiness.

Wandering thoughts

If your thoughts wander and you have difficulty concentrating as you pray, defeat that enemy by praying aloud instead of silently. Putting your thoughts into words and praying them aloud helps you focus your mind on what you're doing. Perhaps that is one of the reasons why Jesus commanded: 'When you pray, *say:* Our Father in heaven' (Luke 11:2 RAV).

Once you learn to defeat interruptions, drowsiness and wandering thoughts, within just a short time the *desire* to pray will have matured into the *discipline* to pray. And as you discipline yourself to pray, that discipline will be transformed into holy *delight*.

Don't worry if some days as you pray you shed no

tears and feel no emotion. Those times when you *feel* the least like praying may be the times you most *need* to pray. Besides, God is moved not so much by your tears and your emotions as he is moved by his Word and by your obedience and tenacity.

Always be sensitive to the Holy Spirit and pray over each request in the manner he directs, for God has sent his Spirit to come to your aid in prayer and plead on your behalf with groanings too deep for words (Romans 8:26). Learn to be sensitive by using your prayer language, praying in the Spirit and listening for the Holy Spirit's promptings.

At times the Spirit will lead you to take verses of Scripture and turn them into petitions or bold declarations of your faith. At other times, you will find yourself weeping and travailing over an urgent need. Sometimes you will break into worshipful singing or laughter as God's peace and joy flood your heart.

Don't try to make any two prayer times identical. Follow the omniscient Holy Spirit's quiet nudges and forceful impressions, for his choices and leadings are never wrong. So be sensitive. Be flexible. Be obedient. Don't grieve the gentle Holy Spirit by demanding your own way.

Pastor B.J. Willhite, our minister of prayer at Church on the Rock who has risen to commune with God early every morning for over thirty years, explains prayer like this: 'Some days you're digging holes. Some days you're planting poles. Some days you're stringing wire. And then one day the circuit is completed, and you make contact!'

God your Father makes this promise: 'When you answer the call to pray, I will begin to meet all your needs.' How about it? Are you ready to make an appointment with God each day to seek his face in prayer? Just name the time and place. He won't be late.

19

Patterns to follow

In Waco, Texas, they did a survey and found there were more Baptists in Waco than people! That's a true story. Most Baptists in Texas — and many others — have probably heard of W.A. Criswell, a patriarch in the Southern Baptist Convention. How I appreciate and love that dear man.

After I had pastored for several years at Church on the Rock, Criswell called and requested that my elders and I come to his office in downtown Dallas. We were surprised and delighted by his invitation to visit First Baptist Church, where he pastors.

We 'small-talked' with this gracious, gentle servant of God for about thirty seconds. Then Criswell turned to me and said, 'I want to ask you a question. Why aren't you a Baptist?'

I was born, raised and educated a Southern Baptist, so I was ready for the greatest rebuke of my life.

Perhaps sensing my apprehension, he phrased the question another way. 'If it were not for the Baptists, son, you couldn't read or write. Why aren't you a Baptist?'

'Dr Criswell,' I began hesitantly, trying to figure out what he was driving at, 'have you got a moment?'

'Yes,' he replied graciously. So I shared my testimony — how Jesus had saved me in the midst of a nervous breakdown in a mental ward, healed me and called me to preach. I told Criswell about reading the red and praying for the power as a student at Dallas Baptist College and how I found myself speaking a language I had never learned after praying, 'Lord, if there's power in this gospel, give it to me!'

I continued sharing with this beloved pastor, telling him of my call to pray and how that call had haunted me until I answered it. I described how I obeyed God and began a church in Rockwall, dedicated to the principle of rising early in the morning, praying and then obeying God's voice.

Not knowing exactly how much Criswell wanted to hear, I hesitated. As I did, he leaned forward and, with tears rolling down his lined cheeks, signalled me to stop. 'That's enough,' he said, not quibbling over our doctrinal differences. Taking my hand in his, he said simply, 'You've done it the Bible way.' Then we wept together for a few moments.

'Dr Criswell,' I asked as I wiped my tears, 'what is *your* secret? You've spent forty successful years in the same church.'

I shouldn't have been surprised at his answer. 'I get up every day and spend the first five hours with God. I spend the first hour in prayer; the next two hours in study; the next hour in meditation; then, in the final hour, I get to thinking about what I ought to do for the rest of the day.'

After the appointment as I walked out of the door, Criswell asked, 'Do you know this man Cho? I've read all his books and heard his tapes, and I'm so intrigued by him.'

I told Criswell that I had met Paul Yonggi Cho and, in fact, was scheduled to preach the very next week in his church in Korea. I promised to tell Cho that Criswell wished to meet him.

That next week I sat beside Cho at a banqueting table. Out of the clear blue he turned to me and asked, 'Do you know this man Criswell? I've read all his books and listened to his tapes.'

Talk about 'holy chemistry'! Then I said, 'Dr Cho, I spoke with Dr Criswell last week, and he said the very same thing about you.'

As soon as I got back to Dallas, I called Criswell and enquired, 'What would you say if I said that Dr Cho would be willing to preach on a Sunday night at First Baptist Church in Dallas?'

Without a moment's hesitation, Criswell replied, 'I'd say, "Praise God, let's do it!"'

So that's how, in the autumn of 1984, I accompanied Cho to First Baptist Church in downtown Dallas on a Sunday night. Cho preached and after the meeting was over, the staff slipped out quickly and put us into a limousine. There I sat with my two pastoral heroes. I wanted to be as quiet as a mouse and take it all in.

Criswell opened the conversation. 'Now, Cho,' he began, 'I've admired you for many years, but I'll be quite frank with you. After reading your books and listening to your tapes, I had concluded that what you've done in Korea was strictly a sociological phenomenon — something that probably couldn't have happened at any other time in history, at any other place in the world. But then I met this lad here.' He gestured towards me.

'So, Lea,' Criswell continued, 'would you tell me how you got it from Seoul, Korea, over here to Texas?'

I cast a knowing glance at Cho, then responded: 'I pray, and I obey!'

Well, I had a glorious time at supper that night because these men of God were so honest, so transparent.

Criswell said, 'Cho, I hear that you pray.'

I should tell you that Cho had preached that morning in our eight o'clock service. Before the service began, my elders and I were in a small prayer room behind the platform interceding when Cho and his assistant, Cha, entered. When I invited them to join us in prayer, Cho replied softly, 'I've prayed. I've already spent three hours in prayer this morning for the service.'

Even so, he and Cha knelt and prayed with us a little

longer. When the service began, Cho ministered under
a powerful anointing. I happen to know that Cho also
spent two more hours in prayer in the afternoon
before going to First Baptist Church that evening to
preach for Criswell. So Criswell was correct: Cho
prays!

That night at supper Criswell jokingly confided,
'Cho, when I pray for fifteen minutes, I feel as if I've
worn God out and worn myself out, too. How can
somebody pray as you pray? How do you do it?'

I'm so glad Cho didn't give Criswell a traditional
Pentecostal answer such as, 'I speak in tongues and
you don't.' Instead, Cho smiled graciously, and said,
'Every morning I get on a "running track" in the Spirit,
and I circle that track. I know when I'm one-fifth of
the way through, two-fifths, four-fifths and then,
finally, I know when I'm done. Then, if I have time,
I run it again and again, just as a runner would circle
a track.'

The conversation continued for some time that
evening. The next morning Cho and I played golf. At
least I played golf. Cho was busy communing with the
Holy Spirit. He would hit the ball, turn, get back in
the cart and not even watch to see where his ball went.
It was the funniest game of golf I have ever played.

Finally, I plucked up courage and asked, 'Dr Cho,
what is the running track you were telling Dr Criswell
about last night?'

I listened in amazement as Cho rapidly described
many of the same principles I had learned about
prayer from the Holy Spirit. Something leapt inside
me in excited confirmation as Cho confided that his
'prayer track' is the Lord's Prayer; the 'laps' he runs
around that track are the six timeless topics of the
model prayer that Jesus gave his disciples.

Did those early disciples follow the prayer pattern
Jesus gave them? Yes, historical literature records that
they did. The early Jewish-Christian document *The*

Didache instructed early Christians to pray the Lord's Prayer three times daily. And Christ's desire for his church hasn't changed.

It is to be a house of purity, prayer, power and perfected praise. At what point are you in that divine progression, clay temple of the Most High God? At which stage will your prayer life be this time next year? Desire? Discipline? Delight? It's your choice.

If you don't begin to pray, you will not be any further along with the Lord next year than you are right now. The Spirit of God longs to teach you to walk in the yoke he has fitted for you.

Everyone wants to change, but change demands desire and discipline before it becomes delightful. There is always the agony of choice before the promise of change. Therefore, we must consciously, deliberately choose to go on with God.

If we pray the Lord's Prayer as it should be prayed, we choose to obey the major messages of Christ's life and ministry.

We sanctify the name of God in our worship and in our walk. We repent, place God's priorities before our own and become a part of his kingdom movement. We set our wills to forgive and to live in right relationship with God and others. We tenaciously pray specific prayers for our daily provision.

Clad in the whole armour of God and encircled by his hedge of protection, we resist temptation and defeat the devil and his evil powers. And we give praise to God our Father who has made us partakers in his kingdom, his power and his glory.

You have my word on it. Something supernatural happens when you take your next step with God. He walked me right out of a psychiatric ward. He led a hippy named Jerry Howell into the ministry. My dad took God's hand and walked away from a life of alcoholism and misery. If you are ready for God to do a new thing in your life, you must take your next step with him.

'Could you not tarry one hour?' Someone is asking you that question right now, and his name is not Henry. His name is Jesus.

20

For the sake of ten

Paul Yonggi Cho once lamented to me: 'Americans will give their money, sing songs, build buildings and preach, but they will not pray.' But, thank God, the Lord is changing all that. The Spirit of intercession, the praying Holy Spirit, is overcoming our flesh.

We are in the first stages of the most life-changing, nation-shaping move of God since the beginning of the world. God is bringing to birth a prayer revival — not a doctrine, not a teaching built around the charisma of men, but a spirit of intercession that is invading the lives of his people. Why? Because the word has gone out: mediation or annihilation.

Who among us is not aware of God's gathering storm of judgment? Towering thunderheads of divine wrath loom on the horizon, and prophetic rumblings of impending calamity reverberate throughout the western world.

Centuries ago, Abraham watched such clouds of calamity collect over Sodom and Gomorrah. And one day the Lord delivered a dreaded message to Abraham's doorstep — in person. From that visit and from the events that transpired, we can distil four principles that enlighten our understanding and inspire our intercession. The principles pertain to the prevailing ignorance of the wicked and to the preserving influence, the persevering intercession and the powerful impact of the righteous.

The prevailing ignorance of the unrighteous

The unrighteous are unaware that God holds inquest

on the moral condition of cities, but Genesis 18:20-21 confirms this awesome fact: 'The Lord said, "The outcry against Sodom and Gomorrah is so great and their sin so grievous that I will go down and see if what they have done is as bad as the outcry that has reached me. If not, I will know."'

Then followed Abraham's eloquent, urgent intercession on behalf of the cities: 'What if there are fifty righteous people in the city? Will you really sweep it away and not spare the place for the sake of the fifty righteous people in it?'

And the Lord said, 'If I find fifty righteous people in the city of Sodom, I will spare the whole place for their sake' (Genesis 18:24, 26).

Four more times, Abraham reverently pleaded with God for the city's welfare, each time lowering the number of righteous people required to stay God's hand, turn judgment and avert destruction. Would the Lord destroy the city if there were forty-five righteous? Forty righteous? Thirty? Twenty?

Abraham wasn't merely haggling with God, who has no pleasure in the death of the wicked (Ezekiel 33:11). Abraham knew God's long-suffering, compassionate nature; therefore, he stood before him and pleaded one last time for mercy. 'What if only ten can be found there?'

And God answered, 'For the sake of ten, I will not destroy it' (Genesis 18:32).

The ungrateful, ungodly inhabitants of Sodom would have been amazed to learn the value the Lord sets on the righteous. The entire city could have been spared for the sake of ten righteous people within its walls; indeed, only Lot, the one righteous man in Sodom, and his family were saved (Genesis 19:15-16).

And if Sodom's inhabitants could have overheard the Lord's assurance to Abraham that if fifty, forty, thirty, twenty or even ten righteous people could be found in Sodom he would not destroy the city, they would have been stunned by this staggering truth: it

is not the presence of evil which brings the mercy and
long-suffering of God to an end; rather, it is the
absence of good.

The preserving influence of the righteous

The haughty enemies of God who undervalue and
persecute those who live 'self-controlled, upright and
godly lives in this present age' are also unaware of the
preserving influence of the righteous (Titus 2:12).

According to Sam Shoemaker, the nineteenth-
century church historian William Lecky credited John
Wesley with saving England from revolution. All
across the island Wesley had set up little companies
of twelve. Each group had a leader, met once a week
and helped hold each other up to Christian standards.[1]

Judge for yourself: Did that small remnant, which
lifted the moral and spiritual level of the nation, keep
England from going the way of France, where in that
same century revolution toppled the government?
What would have happened in France if they had had
a John Wesley or a spiritual revival to preserve it from
decay and destruction?

Remember: God would have spared Sodom for the
sake of ten. Some say this would have been approximately one-tenth of one per cent of the city's
population — just a sprinkling of salt in the midst of
massive decay, a glimmer of light in gross darkness.
Yet, in God's eyes, ten righteous people would have
been sufficient cause to spare Sodom.

The purposeful intercession of the remnant

Abraham's intercession for Sodom was the result of
divine communication: 'The Lord said, "Shall I hide
from Abraham what I am about to do?"' (Genesis
18:17). The Spirit sometimes inspires people to pray
by showing them things to come. God reveals his in-
tentions to his friends, thus inviting their intercession.

[1] *Extraordinary Living for Ordinary Men*, by Samuel Shoemaker, Zondervan,
Grand Rapids, Michigan, 1965

Although God invites our intercession, our prayers must be in line with God's character and his covenant with humankind. Note that when Abraham brought before God the reasons why his request should be granted, the motive behind his intercession was not small, selfish or shortsighted: 'Abraham approached him and said: "Will you sweep away the righteous with the wicked? . . . Will not the Judge of all the earth do right?"' (Genesis 18:23, 25).

God is bound by his nature and by his covenant with humankind; he can do nothing that is not inflexibly righteous. Therefore, Abraham appealed to God to preserve his name and honour before the world. He also pleaded God's perfect justice. God would not destroy the righteous with the wicked, the innocent with the guilty. Was it not better that the wicked be spared mercifully than that the righteous be destroyed unrighteously?

The powerful impact of the righteous

God has given us this unwavering assurance: 'If my people, who are called by my name, will humble themselves and pray and seek my face and turn from their wicked ways, then will I hear from heaven and will forgive their sin and will heal their land' (2 Chronicles 7:14).

But God has also given us this sobering alternative: 'I looked for a man among them who would build up the wall and stand before me in the gap on behalf of the land so that I would not have to destroy it, but I found none. So I will pour out my wrath on them and consume them with my fiery anger, bringing down on their own heads all they have done, declares the Sovereign Lord' (Ezekiel 22:30-31).

The church is sometimes prone to measure influence by numbers of people and money. But we cannot use our arithmetic to estimate the impact of the righteous; God saves by many or by few.

I'm not intimidated to declare to you that God has called me to enlist, instruct, encourage and inspire three hundred thousand believers to pray. On one scale that is a lot more than Sodom's ten, but on another scale it isn't. That is one-tenth of one per cent of the population of the USA. God will not allow a nation to destroy itself if his people will repent over the sins of that nation and seek his face. If we will pray, destruction will be averted and judgment can be turned.

My question is: Will you pledge to pray one hour a day for yourself, your loved ones, the ignorant and the unbelieving? Will you promise to intercede for God's spotted, wrinkled church? That is our only hope. Believe it.

Why not join your prayers with the petitions of thousands of prayer warriors who have already enlisted in this mighty prayer army?

God is setting a mark upon the foreheads of those who sigh and groan for all the abominations of the land (Ezekiel 9:4-6). As in Ezekiel's day, destruction will not come near any person upon whom that mark is set.

May the pledge of God himself echo in our ears and drive us to our knees: 'For the sake of ten, I will not destroy it' (Genesis 18:32).

Prayer guide

1. 'Our Father in heaven, hallowed be your name'

a. Picture Calvary and thank God you can call him Father by virtue of the blood of Jesus

b. Hallow the names of God corresponding with the five benefits in the new covenant, and make your faith declarations:

Benefit	Name	Meaning
Sin	*Jehovah-tsidkenu*	The Lord My Righteousness
	Jehovah-m'kaddesh	The Lord Who Sanctifies
Spirit	*Jehovah-shalom*	The Lord is Peace
	Jehovah-shammah	The Lord is There
Soundness	*Jehovah-rophe*	The Lord Who Heals
Success	*Jehovah-jireh*	The Lord's Provision Shall be Seen
Security	*Jehovah-nissi*	The Lord My Banner
	Jehovah-rohi	The Lord My Shepherd

2. 'Your kingdom come, your will be done'

a. Yourself

b. Your family (partner, children, other family members)

c. Your church (pastor, leadership, faithfulness of the people, harvest)

d. Nation (specific area; local and national political and spiritual leaders; a specific nation)

3. 'Give us today our daily bread'

a. Be in the will of God (prayer life, church, work habits, obedience in giving)

b. Believe that it is God's will to prosper you

c. Be specific

d. Be tenacious

4. 'Forgive us our debts, as we also have forgiven our debtors'

a. Ask God to forgive you

b. Forgive and release others

c. Set your will to forgive those who sin against you

5. 'Lead us not into temptation, but deliver us from the evil one'

a. Put on the whole armour of God, the Lord Jesus Christ
- [ ] Belt of truth
- [ ] Breastplate of righteousness
- [ ] Feet equipped with the readiness of the gospel of peace
- [ ] Shield of faith
- [ ] Helmet of salvation
- [ ] Sword of the Spirit which is the word *(rhema)* of God
- [ ] Praying always in the Spirit

b. Pray a hedge of protection. (The Lord is your refuge, your fortress, your God; in him you will trust)
- [ ] Because you have made the Lord your dwelling
- [ ] Because you have set your love upon him
- [ ] Because you acknowledge his name

6. 'Yours is the kingdom and the power and the glory for ever'

a. Make your faith declarations

b. Return to praise

Good books from Harvestime by David Matthew

A Sound Mind
God-governed thought life

In an easy-to-read style, David Matthew shows how to conquer depression, master painful memories, develop a healthy self-image and build up a bank of good thoughts. A feast of down-to-earth spirituality for all who want to say goodbye for ever to mental confusion.

ISBN 0 947714 23 5 £2.25

Dead Dreams Can Live!
Your hopes fulfilled

God-given dreams inspire us. Have you written off your dreams as wishful thinking or crazy, youthful idealism? Has your dream died? It's not too late for things to change. Your dream can live again!

ISBN 0 947714 19 7 £1.95

Church Adrift
Where in the world are we going?

Today's church, to put it mildly, is a shambles, a disaster area. Who can blame the man in the street for regarding it as totally irrelevant? David Matthew takes a radical look at the history of the Christian church and suggests some dynamic means of improvement.

ISBN 0 551 01275 7 £2.95

Belonging
Local church membership

Christians need to belong! But what does belonging involve? This simple, Bible-based course will point new Christians in the right direction.

ISBN 0 947714 59 6 £1.95